Mexican Picaresque
Narratives

Mexican Picaresque Narratives

Periquillo and Kin

Timothy G. Compton

Lewisburg
Bucknell University Press
London: Associated University Presses

Associated University Presses
440 Forsgate Drive
Cranbury, NJ 08512

Associated University Presses
16 Barter Street
London WC1A 2AH, England

Associated University Presses
P.O. Box 338, Port Credit
Mississauga, Ontario
Canada L5G 4L8

Library of Congress Cataloging-in-Publication Data

Compton, Timothy G., 1960–
    Mexican picaresque narratives : Periquillo and kin / Timothy G. Compton.
        p.   cm.
    Includes bibliographical references (p.   ) and index.
    ISBN 0-8387-5348-5 (alk. paper)
    1. Picaresque literature, Mexican—History and criticism.
2. Mexican fiction—History and criticism.   I. Title.
PQ7207.P53C7   1997
863'.087—dc21   97-451
                                                                   CIP

*Dedicated to Merlin D.
and Avon A. Compton*

Contents

Preface

Wherein the author reveals his notion of the wily term "picaresque," after which he sets forth the mode by which he will examine each of the Mexican narratives of this study.

Defining a genre or subgenre is an impossible but very useful task. Scholars and critics inevitably disagree on definitions and classifications. Some writers delight in producing texts which seem to challenge and defy notions of genre. Is *La Celestina* a novel or a play? Although definitive resolution of this question will never occur, asking the question and attempting to find an answer help us focus on details which reveal a great deal about the nature of the text.

The existence of "picaresque" narratives can hardly be challenged—critics have referred to them as such for many years. *Lazarillo de Tormes, Guzmán de Alfarache* and *El buscón* constitute classics of the subgenre, and many other narratives belong by almost universal consent, but critics see some texts as picaresque while others do not. *Tom Jones,* for example, has a picaresque plot with a picaresque protagonist but lacks the first-person narrator of the picaresque classics mentioned above. Critics differ over whether it qualifies as picaresque, but the process of classifying it reveals a great deal about it.

Many critics have attempted to identify what makes a work picaresque. Their differing terminologies, approaches, and emphases attest to the difficulty in defining a genre. I do not seek to resolve this ongoing debate, but to examine a group of Mexican narratives which seem to fall under the classification of picaresque either wholly or in part. Rather than add to the growing list of picaresque definitions, I here yield to the definitions given by some of the leading theorists on the subject. I have found three approaches to the problem at hand especially helpful. The first is the classic "Toward a Definition of the Picaresque" by Claudio Guillén.[1] In his discussion of the pure picaresque genre he focuses largely on the picaro and the narrative stance. The second is *The Picaresque Novel* by Stuart Miller.[2] This approach "constructs an ideal type" based on eight standard picaresque novels. Miller focuses largely on the structure of picaresque narratives and thematic patterns therein. Last is Ulrich Wicks's "The Nature of Picaresque Narrative: A Modal Approach."[3] This work, as can be inferred from its title, departs from Robert Scholes's ideas on fictional modes. He defines the "essential picaresque situation" by a set of characteristics which include a certain narrative situation and structure, as well as a certain type of protagonist and thematic motifs. The three approaches mentioned here overlap and draw on one another. I have extracted and synthesized the following points as ones that seem to be basic to and easily observed in picaresque narratives.

1) *Episodic Plot.* Episodes structure picaresque narratives, with no cause-effect relationships occurring between episodes. Thus, characters appear then disappear in rapid succession, rarely to be remembered again. Constant changes from milieu to milieu often accentuate this structure. Normally, the picaro himself provides the only common link between episodes.[4]

2) *Dizzying Rhythm.* The episodic nature of picaresque narratives lends itself to a vertiginous pace. Events occur in "strikingly short compass." This bedazzles both the reader and the picaro.[5]

3) *Fate Rules Supreme.* The picaro stands unable to control his circumstances for any extended period of time. Chaos, fate, destiny and luck always reign in his life. At times he encounters good luck, but it never lasts for long, thus leading to what Wicks refers to as the "Sisyphus rhythm."[6]

4) *Bodily Violence.* On occasion horrible and sometimes disgusting events befall the picaro. These mishaps take their toll on the picaro in a direct, physical way. The picaro does not "deserve" these calamities—they do not constitute punishment for any particular misdeed. Wicks calls this the "grotesque or horrible incident motif."[7]

5) *The Picaro.* Identifying what makes a protagonist a "picaro" is a particularly sticky business. Bjornson, Parker, and others have written books that deal entirely with picaros and what qualifies a character as such. The following are suggestions from Miller, Wicks, and Guillén.

5a) *A Single Protagonist.* Guillén states that "every roguish novel worthy of its salt could be described by a single name."[8] The presence of a single, antiheroic protagonist is absolutely indispensable for a work to be truly picaresque.

5b) *Uncommon Origins.* "The circumstances surrounding the picaro's entrance into the world are often unusual and thus they are omens of a sort."[9] Some picaros never learn the identity of their mother. Still more lack the same knowledge regarding their father. Some come from an underworld background. The picaro is almost always an orphan in either a literal or a figurative sense. He enjoys no family relationships. Thus, from his beginnings the picaro finds himself thrust into chaos and instability.[10]

5c) *Cunning*. The picaro is a "pragmatic, unprincipled, resilient, solitary figure who just manages to survive in his chaotic landscape, but who, in the ups and downs, can also put that world very much on the defensive."[11] Guillén states that he is "not all picardía—the slyness of the trickster who lives on his wits, just short of delinquency if possibly he can. Guile and wile are only his offensive weapons. A stoical good humor is his defensive one."[12] The picaro survives no matter how difficult the situation.

5d) *Protean Form*. The picaro typically acts in a number of different roles. He can serve a series of masters or wear numerous professional masks and costumes. "There is no part a picaro won't play." In his adaptability, the picaro's personality never becomes clearly defined. Paradoxically, in the process of becoming "everyman" he becomes no man.[13]

5e) *Alienation*. Guillén speaks of the picaro as a "half-outsider."[14] Although he interacts within society he never fully integrates into it. An absence of love and loyalty in his life lead him to remain detached from any person or thing, and he becomes what Miller calls an "unanchored self."[15] At times the picaro seems on the verge of integration, but the Sisyphus rhythm prevails and he finds himself further alienated.

5f) *Internal Instability*. Given the picaro's chaotic origins, Protean form, and alienation, internal chaos naturally results. He is unable to carry out his decisions. Sudden impulses, curiosity, and mischievousness rule him rather than resolve and determination.[16]

5g) *A Philosophical Bent*. This characteristic stems in part from the narrative situation as well as from the picaro's curiosity and observant nature. Because the picaro tells the story after it takes place, he tends to comment on the events in a philosophical way. His insightful reflections on society, politics, and human nature indicate an active and attentive mind.[17]

6) *The First-person Point of View*. Guillén sees the first-person point of view as absolutely essential for a work to be truly

picaresque. Because the picaro narrates the events retrospectively, he is once again fragmented, in this case into a narrating self and an experiencing self. This situation adds to the reader's view of the picaro's interior instability, assures that the work will be partial and prejudiced, and provides an excellent vehicle for irony. The reader can never fully trust the narrative because of the picaro's penchant and talent for invention and falsification.[18]

7)   *An Unkind, Chaotic World.* The world the picaro lives in is hostile and unforgiving. Therefore, many critics consider the picaresque classics to be "realistic." The society portrayed matches the picaro himself in chaos. Miller claims the picaro merely reflects the world in which he lives.[19]

8)   *Physical Survival.* "There is a general stress on the material level of existence or of subsistence, on sordid facts, hunger, money."[20] Despite his occasional philosophical narrative style, the issue of the picaro's next meal constitutes an unending concern. He employs much of his cunning precisely to fulfill this need.[21]

9)   *A Vast Gallery of Human Types.* In his wanderings and travels, a picaro manages to interact with an impressive array of people from varying social classes, professions, regions, and nationalities. The picaresque plot structure dictates that the characters are almost always types. Although they cannot be well developed, their presence and presentation provide some of the most memorable moments of picaresque narratives.[22]

Chapter 1 of this manuscript provides a panoramic view of the history of the picaresque in Mexico. It deals primarily with texts which are only partially picaresque, thus establishing a context for the more fully picaresque texts examined in chapters 2–9. A single Mexican text corresponds to each of these chapters, wherein my critical strategy involves a four-step process. First, I comment on the narrative's chronological place in Mexican literature, especially with regard to other picaresque novels. Second, I remark on the criticism the work has received. Third, I look at the text's elements by lining it up against basic elements of the picaresque stated above. Last, I examine the narratives through analyses of language, narrative techniques, codes, character analysis, or whatever approach I find illuminating with regard to the text. Chapter 10 provides observations, based on the foregoing analyses, on relationships between the eight narratives and the manner in which each represents a unique creation.

With the exception of the chapter on *La vida inútil de Pito Pérez,* all translations in this book are my own.

I gratefully acknowledge the helpful comments of John Brushwood, Jon Vincent, and Diana Alvárez in the early stages of this manuscript. The mentoring influence of Professor Brushwood, Joel Hancock, and Merlin Compton are patent in the ideas and approaches of this book, and I hope this book serves as a small tribute to them. The fellowship awarded me by the University of Kansas was most opportune. I appreciate the love and encouragement I have received from my wife, Virginia, in this project, and in all things worthwhile. Finally, thanks to my children for their invigorating influence.

Mexican Picaresque
Narratives

1

A Survey of Partially Picaresque Narratives

Wherein a survey is made of Mexican narratives that, although not fully picaresque, feature prominent elements of the subgenre, thereby establishing a context for the eight texts examined in chapters two through nine of this study.

THIS STUDY EXAMINES AT LENGTH EIGHT NARRATIVES, ALthough by no means do they represent the only Mexican texts containing picaresque elements or flavor. Depending on the criteria used to define the subgenre, some critics could classify some of them as full members of the family. The eight narratives analyzed at length in chapters two through nine were selected in light of the model established in this study's preface. The present chapter lessens the gaps between the eight by examining, albeit briefly, many of Mexico's additional narratives containing noteworthy picaresque characteristics.[1]

A number of texts besides *Naufragios* [*Shipwrecks,* 1542] from the period of discovery and conquest have attributes suggesting close kinship to the picaresque family.[2] The "Carta segunda" (Second letter) of Hernán Cortés's *Cartas de relación de la conquista de México* [*Letters on the Conquest of Mexico*], written in 1520, has several decidedly picaresque qualities.[3] To begin with, Cortés narrates with the first-person, retrospective point of view. Furthermore, he addresses the king in the same way that *Lazarillo de Tormes* addresses "vuestra merced" [your highness]. Cortés acts as a picaro in several ways, particularly in the astounding cunning he and his handful of fellow Spaniards utilize to conquer the Aztecs against overwhelming odds. His skillful manipulation of Malinche, Moctezuma, opposing Indian groups, and even his own men for his own purposes matches the genius of any picaro. Moreover, he cleverly tells his story in such a way as to lead the king to overlook his military disobedience to Pánfilo de Narváez, the king's representative. Like a picaro, he becomes completely alienated from those around him. Not only does he mistrust and maintain emotional distance from all factions of the Native Americans he meets, including Malinche, but he does the same with his fellow Europeans. Even though he performs maneuvers in company with his men and often with many Indians, in the text he rarely refers to events in the "nosotros" [we] form, opting instead for the "yo" [I] form. Such avoidance of the first-person plural constitutes linguistic evidence of his alienation. Physical survival, an unkind, chaotic world, and the presentation of many human types also form part of Cortés's narrative. Thus, as with Cabeza de Vaca's narrative, although it predates the classic picaresque novels, Cortés's letter shares many similarities with the tradition.

Although to a lesser extent, Bernal Díaz de Castillo's account of the conquest, published as *Historia verdadera de la conquista de la Nueva España* [*True History of the Conquest of New Spain*] in 1632, more than fifty years after his death, also contains features of the picaresque.[4] Díaz's account surpasses Cortés's in its picaresque nature, in its episodic structure, and in a gallery of human types both more extensive and better developed as individuals. As in Cortés's account, Díaz recounts the story using the first-person point of view, and physical survival is a recurring theme. On the other hand, whereas in the *Cartas de relación* Cortés clearly presents himself as the narrative's main character, Díaz does not in *Historia verdadera*. Although in some episodes Díaz certainly highlights himself and his role in the conquest, unlike the picaro, he does not alone provide coherence to the narrative.

Infortunios de Alonso Ramírez [*Misfortunes of Alonso Ramírez,* 1690] stands alone as the only significantly picaresque narrative in Mexican prose between *Historia verdadera* and *El Periquillo Sarniento* [*The Itching Parrot,* 1816].[5] José Joaquín Fernández de Lizardi distinguished himself not only by the quality of his narratives that belong to the picaresque family, but also as the most prolific in number of texts. Lizardi flanked the *Periquillo* with another full member of the family, *Don Catrín de la Fachenda* [*Mr. Dandy Conceited,* written 1819, published 1832] and *La Quijotita y su prima* [*Quijotita and Her Cousin*], which has minor kinship in the subgenre.

In a strict sense, *La educación de las mujeres o la Quijotita y su prima* [*The Training of Women, or Quijotita and Her Cousin*], published in 1818, has none of the picaresque characteristics set forth in the preface of this study.[6] In a loose way, Pomposa, whose nickname is Quijotita, has the potential to be a female picaro in the cast of Catrín. She is as spoiled and presumptuous as her cousin, Pudenciana, is modest and virtuous. A touch of picaresque satire and flavor surfaces periodically in the text, especially in the presentation of character types. Nonetheless, critics associate the book with the picaresque family primarily because its author is Mexico's most prominent cultivator of the subgenre.

Applying the term picaresque to any narrative written in Mexico between Fernández de Lizardi and Rubén Romero merits a strong qualifying explanation. Some of the literary "-isms" of the period, namely realism, naturalism and "costumbrismo," led narrative away from the picaresque in several ways. First, episodic structure wherein a single protagonist links the episodes stepped aside for a more complex, interwoven structure in which many characters tie the plot together. Second, third-person narrative point of view almost completely displaced first-person point of view. Third, in place of fate and chance being major factors in the plot, realist narratives seek to establish cause-and-effect relationships. Conversely, these same "-isms" manifest other attributes associated with the picaresque. For example, the less-than-perfect settings that realism and naturalism often highlight echo the "unkind, chaotic world" of the picaresque. "Costumbrista" sketches do not limit themselves to the description of customs only, but lend themselves to the portrayal of types as well, thus reminiscent of the presentation of "a vast gallery of human types" in the picaresque. Thus, although the "-isms" of the nineteenth century do not lend themselves to the cultivation of fully picaresque works, some of the narratives do have characteristics and/or flavor of the subgenre.

Tras un mal nos vienen ciento [*After One Misfortune Come a Hundred*], published in 1839 by Ignacio Rodríguez Galván, is an enjoyable little piece with interesting variations on several picaresque elements.[7] Even though it has no formal divisions, the story's structure functions like a picaresque narrative in that the protagonist, Don Gregorio Ventrículo, holds the story together. In this tale, however, Don Gregorio is not even vaguely a picaro, but rather an established, well-to-do, older bachelor. Instead, picaresque types victimize the protagonist. These types include a boy swindler posing as a salesman, a coachman who charges him an exorbitant fee for a minimal ride, some furniture movers who at first unwittingly and then uncaringly bruise him as they work, several overly talkative acquaintances who delay him, and so forth. These misfortunes and many others befall Don Gregorio as he tries to make good on a dinner appointment. Thus, as in picaresque novels, hunger serves as a backdrop to the action, and intensifies as the text progresses. Ironically, the eventual meal falls far short of satisfactory. In a striking variation from picaresque conventions, the story uses an almost completely dialogued form. This technique gives the narrative nearly dramatic life and avoids a complete break with the first-person point of view by giving the protagonist some voice.

El fistol del diablo [*The Devil's Tie Pin*], published in 1845 and 1846 by Manuel Payno, and *Astucia,* published in 1865 by Luis G. Inclán, share similar characteristics with the picaresque.[8] Both have episodic plot structure, so it should not surprise us that both appeared first as installments in newspapers. Nevertheless, they do not rely on a single protagonist to link the episodes, but rather have a large number of characters who act throughout extended sections of the text. While *Astucia* has a clear protagonist with minor picaresque traits, such as Protean form, the central figure of *El fistol del diablo* does not dominate the text and is not a picaro in any sense. The outstanding characteristic of each book is the presentation of numerous characters, forming a vast, although rarely satiric, gallery of human types. Very few picaresque characteristics appear in any of the books of this period.

Monja y casada, virgen y mártir [*Nun and Married, Virgin and Martyr*], and *Martín Garatuza,* form a two-part historical novel published by Vicente Riva Palacio in 1868.[9] The novel's most prominent picaro type, in spite of having the second volume of the work named after him, does not provide the novel with structural unity. He displays occasional cunning in his chaotic surroundings, but the text focuses on intrigues and scheming in early seventeenth-century Mexico rather than on Garatuza and his dealings.

Several of the short sketches which make up José T. de Cuéllar's *La linterna mágica* [*The Magic Lantern*] have marked picaresque flavor. They excel in satiric presentation of human types, as suggested in the following titles: *Las jamonas* [*The Buxom Middle-aged Women*], *Los mariditos* [*The Little Husbands*], and *Ensalada de pollos* [*Chicken Salad*]. In spite of its name, *Historia de Chucho el Ninfo* [*The Story of Chucho the Dandy*], published in 1871, does not focus exclusively on Chucho's story.[10] Since he disappears from the story's focus during large portions of the text, the structure is not even remotely picaresque. Chucho qualifies as a picaro in his illegitimacy, his gross irresponsibility, his penchant for donning costumes and personalities, and his renowned cunning with women. In spite of the presence of a picaro, the text most closely resembles the picaresque in its entertaining presentation of an alcoholic priest, a spoiling mother, naive daughters, and so forth, in a satiric gallery of human types.

Memorias de un muerto [*Memoirs of a Dead Man*], published by Manuel Balbontín in 1874, features a narrative situation approximating that of the picaresque.[11] As the title would suggest, Pascual Pintó Pasos, the author's deceased friend, uses a first-person narrative point of view to write his memoirs, some of which deal with life in Hell, which happens to be the planet Jupiter. Strong picaresque flavor imbues the narrative pretext, and some of the items narrated.

Novelas mexicanas [*Mexican Novels*], published by Emilio Rabasa in 1887 and 1888, constitute a set of four full-length novels linked by their narrator, Juan Quiñones.[12] In the first novel he acts as a soldier, in the second as a student, and in the last two as a journalist. Thus, role playing, occasional flashes of cunning, a sometimes philosophical bent, and a tendency toward alienation make the narrator a sort of picaro. The text uses a first-person narrative point of view, presents a small gallery of the town's types, and paints a most unkind society. Most importantly, the novels feature heavy doses of satire with regard to politics and journalism.

Pacotillas [*Shoddy Goods*], published by Porfirio Parra in 1900, lacks almost all of the formal picaresque characteristics set forth in the preface of this study.[13] Nonetheless, three things make it noteworthy for this study. First, several picaro types populate its pages. Second, many characters have colorful nicknames which seem appropriate to picaresque novels. Third, the satiric intent of the book gives it a picaresque flavor. Thus, despite its non-episodic structure, third-person narrative point of view, and its lack of a dominant picaro protagonist, it seems to have kinship with the picaresque family.

El señor gobernador [*Mr. Governor*], published in 1901 by Manuel H. San Juan, features political satire.[14] Although the Díaz regime did not bear fruit in picaresque novels per se, for obvious reasons political satire found voice. The text uses the first-person point of view, but the narrator is not the protagonist. The governor constitutes the book's protagonist, as the book's title suggests. Like a picaro, the governor is self-serving and manipulative, and he unifies the text's structure, albeit not alone. Also like a picaro, in spite of his high visibility and being constantly surrounded by people, he suffers alienation from fellow beings because they treat him not as a person but as a politician. In fact, shortly after leaving office he falls into oblivion. Many of the people on Aceituno's staff have humorous or suggestive names, such as Bermejo (Bright Red) Dr. Remigio Chirona [Dr. Jailbird], Modesto Rapiña [Modest Pillage], the state treasurer, and Rodríguez Istiércol [Rodríguez Manure]. Thus, we enjoy a satiric gallery of governmental types.

Avant-garde tendencies and the revolution dominated the narratives of the first forty years of the twentieth century. Although some of the experimentation of the avant-garde shares a certain spirit of cunning with the picaresque, no narrative between *El señor gobernador* and *La vida inútil de Pito Pérez* [*The Futile Life of Pito Pérez,* published in 1938] incorporates noteworthy picaresque characteristics.[15] Before Rubén Romero's novel, as has been detailed herein, the picaresque had become nearly extinct. Over a century had passed since the publication of *Don Catrín de la Fachenda,* the previous fully picaresque novel. Fully developed picaros became rare, the first-person point of view almost disappeared, and the episodic structure in its pure form ceased to exist. Even the picaresque spirit seems to have faded from narratives written in the first part of this century.

In light of the foregoing literary scenario, the proliferation since 1938 of narratives with a great many picaresque traits seems rather surprising. Surely the skyrocketing number of all varieties of novels in Mexico since 1940 constitutes one factor but does not alone explain the resurgence of the picaresque. José Rubén Romero's success with *La vida inútil* also contributes, but neither does it explain the phenomenon. In the era since its publication, many texts seem to have moved away from the concept of focusing on entire groups or networks of people, as in realism and many narratives with social orientation. Rather, a great many narratives feature one dominating character surrounded by many minor characters, as in *Pedro Páramo* (1955) and *La muerte de Artemio Cruz* [*The Death of Artemio Cruz,* published 1962], to name but two prominent representatives of this tendency.[16] The step from this type of narrative to the picaresque is a minor structural one and has been taken many times in the last five decades.

El Canillitas [*The Shin Bone Man,* 1941] appeared within a few years of *La vida inútil* and in some ways remains one of Mexico's purest picaresque narratives.[17] Four other narratives with prominent picaresque elements came into print during the decade of the forties, making it Mexico's most prolific decade for the picaresque to date. In 1944 Jesús R. Guerrero published *Los olvidados* [*The Forgotton Ones*].[18] Carol Blackburn describes it as "[a] pessimistic novel of the Mexican Revolution which prostitutes a picaresque tale in the name of propaganda."[19] Although the novel does not have a clear-cut protagonist, one prominent character is a picaro in several ways. Abandoned early in life, he grew up in a brothel, plays multiple roles, and survives thanks to his cunning both within and outside the bounds of the law.

Quince uñas y Casanova, aventureros [*Fifteen Nails and Casanova, Adventurers*], a monumental, two-volume work published by Leopoldo Zamora Plowes in 1945, carries the subtitle *Novela histórica picaresca* [*Historical Picaresque Novel*].[20] The two characters mentioned in the title make reference to two picaresque types, the real-life general, Santa Anna, and the fictional Juan Jacobo Casanova. Although not the novel's protagonist, Casanova is more picaro than Santa Anna. Casanova links the complex, interwoven plot, yet its structure is not episodic in the strict picaresque sense. Casanova's aim to try to get as far as possible with the least possible effort seems to guide Santa Anna's life as well.[21] Both are self-serving opportunists who are willing to take any pose, play any role, resort to any trick, and claim allegiance to any cause if they think it will benefit them. Hundreds of characters populate the truly vast gallery of human types, most of whom embrace the same self-serving philosophy of life as Casanova. Doctors, women, common soldiers, military leaders, dramatists, and poets constitute but a few of the types targeted by the text. Although *Quince uñas* is not fully picaresque, it is a truly outstanding narrative.

Garambullo: Historia de un pícaro sin fortuna [*Garambullo: Story of a Luckless Picaro*], published in 1945 by Enrique García Campos, does not fully live up to its subtitle.[22] Carol Blackburn calls it "a costumbrista work picaresque in structure."[23] Garambullo is an adult character who links the episodes of the narrative in the manner of the picaresque. Nonetheless, the narrative does not focus on the protagonist in typical picaresque situations, but in his reformation. Secondary characters, though stereotypes, have none of the satire characteristic of the picaresque.

Río humano [*Human River*], published by Rogelio Barriga Rivas in 1949, professes no family tie to the *Periquillo*.[24] Nevertheless, the structure and narrative situation resemble picaresque conventions. Structurally, the text parallels *Tras un mal nos vienen ciento* in that, though not a picaro, the protagonist alone ties the novel's episodes and characters together. Using the first-person point of view, the protagonist/narrator tells of his experiences while working at a police detention center complete with degrading physical conditions and chaotic atmosphere. The book's title accurately suggests the presentation of a river of human types. However, unlike most picaresque texts, in this one characters receive sympathetic rather than satiric portraits.

Tata Lobo [*Father Wolf*], published in 1952 by Ermilo Abreu Gómez, has many of the major elements thought of as picaresque.[25] It has a simple, episodic plot and a protagonist/picaro in an unkind, chaotic world populated by a cast of character types with ridiculous names. Nonetheless, the novel seems not to belong fully to the *Periquillo*'s literary subfamily, perhaps because it merely uses some of the possibilities offered by the picaresque as a literary genre as an excuse to draw "costumbrista" sketches.[26]

El hombre que fue dos [*The Man Who Was Two Men*), published by José Valdovinos Garza in 1963, features a protagonist with many of the raw materials defining a picaro.[27] He alone rules the text's action, has uncommon origins (he was "born" a second time by surviving a vicious fall from a horse), survives only through repeated shows of cunning, exercises several professions, and plays several roles. Furthermore, he lives in a chaotic world populated by a limited but interesting gallery of military and political types. Nonetheless, the text lacks the structure and narrative voice typical of the picaresque, as well as a picaresque rhythm, violence, and focus on survival. Its tone lacks completely the spunk of the subgenre.

Two of the cornerstone narratives of the "Onda," *La tumba* and *Gazapo,* have prominent picaresque characteristics.[28] José Agustín published *La tumba: revelaciones de un adolescente* [*The Tomb: Revelations of an Adolescent*] in 1964. This book uses the first-person point of view, which had overwhelmingly given way to third-person narratives for many years. Gabriel Guía, the protagonist/narrator, does not come from the lower classes as do most picaros, but from the upper classes of Mexico City. Like a picaro, he is completely alienated from the people around him—a striking fact since during much of the book he describes his quest for physical love. Ironically, after each sexual encounter he feels progressively more alone and humiliated. His speech, often laced with pointed double meanings, reveals his penchant for chicanery. Though the text itself lacks many of the structural elements typical of the picaresque, such as the lack of a gallery of human types and an inadequate variety of situations for the protagonist, *La tumba*'s youthful narrator fits in with the subgenre.

Gustavo Sainz's *Gazapo* [*Young Rabbit*], published in 1965, also uses a first-person point of view to narrate the tale. Its protagonist, too, is an alienated adolescent who resorts to cunning in a variety of situations, among them his amorous pursuit of Gisela and the creation of the narrative. The small circle of friends surrounding the narrator comes across as a small gallery of youthful, human types.

Four years after *Gazapo,* Elena Poniatowska published *Hasta no verte Jesús mío* [*Until I Don't See You, Jesus*].[29] Thus, 1969 marks the year that a woman writer in Mexico tried her hand at the picaresque. The book's protagonist, Jesusa Palancares, is the most developed female picaro in Mexican literature.

Chin-Chin el teporocho [*Chin-Chin the Teporocho*], published in 1972 by Armando Ramírez, lacks the classic picaresque episodic structure.[30] The text follows the ups and downs of the relationship between Rogelio González and Michele rather than showing Rogelio in a variety of places and situations. On the other hand, Rogelio, whose nickname is the title of the book, is a full-blown, developed picaro, who dominates the text as its only protagonist. Like the traditional picaro he tells his own story in a retrospective, first-person point of view. Orphaned at age eight, he lives with his aunt and uncle in a poor, chaotic part of Mexico City. As a result, he learns early to scrap and use his wiles to survive. Although for a time he works in a supermarket, he lacks the internal stability to keep the job. He later peddles marijuana, but only for a short while. In spite of his developing relationship with Michele, he experiences loneliness and alienation. When he finally marries her, he does so not out of love but because she is pregnant. After a miscarriage, their unhappy, shaky marriage crumbles. He turns to alcohol and subsequently becomes a "teporocho," an alcoholic in the lower-class neighborhoods in Mexico City. The process of alienation has become complete: "ser teporocho es llegar a ser nadie" [being a teporocho is to become no one at all].[31]

Gustavo Sainz's third novel, *La princesa del palacio de hierro* [*The Princess of the Iron Palace*], published in 1974, features a woman narrator's voice—that of the "princess" mentioned in the book's title.[32] She is a female picaro of sorts—although she comes from a seemingly stable family situation, she is a very unstable, alienated, self-serving person, willing to resort to trickery to get her way. The text features a completely picaresque gallery of the offbeat human types in the narrator's friends. The group includes some with colorful names such as Guapo Guapo [Handsome Handsome], La Vestida de Hombre [The Cross-Dressed Woman], La Tapatía Grande [The Big Woman From Jalisco], and La Tapatía Chica [The Small Woman From Jalisco]. The flamboyant nature of these characters far exceeds their showy names.

In 1979, the same year in which *El Chanfalla* appeared, Luis Zapata published *Las aventuras, desventuras y sueños de Adonís García, El vampiro de la colonia Roma* [*The Adventures, Misadventures, and Dreams of Adonís García, The Vampire of the Roma Neighborhood*].[33] The protagonist in this novel is homosexual, and his homosexual history and activities constitute its main concern.

The narrative structure is absolutely episodic in the picaresque sense—Adonís García is the only consistent link between episodes. He tells his own story in a retrospective, first-person point of view. Left without parents in his early teens, and feeling doubly alone because of his homosexual tendencies, he goes to Mexico City and becomes a *vampiro,* or homosexual prostitute. He eventually turns to alcohol and drugs and despite many relationships both in and out of his profession, he feels no love or emotional support from anyone. The narrators in this novel and *Chin-Chin el teporocho* endure more loneliness and alienation than any of their Mexican counterparts. The protagonists of *La tumba, Gazapo,* and *La princesa del palacio de hierro* also suffer from extreme loneliness, which suggests a relationship between sexual obsession and alienation. In addition to emotional yearning, Adonís occasionally suffers from hunger and usually lives in shabby surroundings. Unlike most picaresque novels, this narrative lacked ironic or satiric tone. Adonís García, despite his several picaresque traits, does not belong among picaros.

Sobre esta piedra [*Upon This Rock*], published in 1981 by Carlos Eduardo Turón, follows the pattern of the narratives just discussed in its first-person narrative point of view and an alienated protagonist/narrator living in an unkind, chaotic world.[34] The main action in the novel involves its narrator, Pedro Jiménez, trying to avoid coming to justice for a murder he committed. He encounters corruption in a wide variety of people and places. More than his recent counterparts, he has a penchant for philosophizing, but he seems totally lacking in cunning and picaresque charm. Furthermore, the structure is not episodic.

Arráncame la vida [*Wrench my Life From Me*], published by Angeles Mastretta in 1985, features a largely episodic plot linked primarily by the narrative's protagonist and narrator, Catalina Guzmán.[35] Thus, the novel uses a first-person narrative point of view. Catalina suffers alienation, and her personality seems based almost entirely on her husband's public/political standing. Like a picara, she manages to survive through her cunning. *Arráncame* introduces an intriguing cast of public figures, including an irreverent view of the Mexican president Manuel Avila Camacho, referred to by the narrator as Fito or the fat president.

Finally, *El general Hilachas* [*General Threadbare*], published in 1985 by José Madrigal Mora, begins with a monologue from the title character that seems to promise the reader a full-fledged picaresque novel.[36] However, after several delicious pages of monologue General Hilachas concedes the narrative voice to an omniscient third-person narrator. A homeless, mentally imbalanced veteran of the Revolution, orphaned at age three, the "general" battles constantly to find his next meal, wears inadequate clothing, suffers bug bites, finds abuse at the hands of society, and has occasional flashes of lucidity on social themes. However, these picaresque traits do not make up for his lack of cunning, Protean form, and instability. Neither is the plot episodic—General Hilachas even disappears during several of the book's later chapters. Despite its picaresque beginning, *El general Hilachas* falls far short of actually joining fully the picaresque family. Admirably, it examines with compassion some of life's marginalized, oft-overlooked inhabitants.

This survey has shown in a very abbreviated form that Mexico boasts numerous narratives featuring prominent picaresque elements. It has made patent the resilience of the subgenre and the usefulness of its conventions in creating literature, since picaresque conventions have surfaced in every era of its narrative writing. Clearly the eight narratives studied in detail hereafter do not stand alone in their tendencies—they merely represent pinnacles in the use of picaresque traits in Mexican narratives.

2

Naufragios

Wherein Cabeza de Vaca's Naufragios *is shown to represent the type of text that reveals a reality so extraordinary as to render fictionalization unnecessary, thus providing at least a partial explanation for the dearth of novels in Spanish America during the Colonial Era, after which its divers picaresque elements are pointed out and illustrated, leading to the hypothesis that travel narratives share close kinship with the picaresque subgenre and therefore* Naufragios *is a forebear of Mexican picaresque novels.*

MORE THAN ONE HISTORIAN OF SPANISH-AMERICAN LITERATURE has tried to explain the absence of novels during the colonial era.[1] However, no one disputes the fact that some of Spanish America's most fascinating narratives emerged prior to Independence. The era of discovery and conquest bore plentiful fruit in this regard, easily evidenced by consulting any anthology of Spanish American literature. In his famous speech delivered before the Swedish Academy prior to receiving the Nobel prize for literature, Gabriel García Márquez acknowledged that many of these narratives "even then contained the seeds of our present-day novels. . . ."[2] I believe that such histories, one of which García Márquez calls "a strictly accurate account that nonetheless resembles a venture into fantasy," constitute a major reason for the absence of the "novel" in Colonial Spanish America.[3] The New World's overwhelming reality rendered illogical, unthinkable, and unnecessary any notion of transforming it into fiction.

García Márquez referred specifically in his speech to *Naufragios* by Alvar Núñez Cabeza de Vaca. It was published with the title *Relación* in 1542, just seven years after Cabeza de Vaca completed the adventures he narrates therein.[4] It has stirred the interest of many people in many disciplines. Much of the attention given to the text stems from its historical value. In the preface to his translation of the work, Cyclone Covey touches on both the work's appeal as an exceptional story and the unique historical position held by Cabeza de Vaca and the other survivors of his expedition:

Four out of a land-force of 300 men—by wits, stamina and luck—found their way back to civilization after eight harrowing years and roughly 6,000 miles over mostly unknown reaches of North America. They were the first Europeans to see—and live to record—the interior of Florida, Texas, New Mexico, Arizona and northernmost Mexico; the 'possum and the buffalo, the Mississippi and the Pecos; pine-nut mash and mesquite-bean flour; and a long string of Indian tribes whose Stone age cultures had never before been intruded by Europeans.[5]

Covey goes on to indicate that scholars of archeology, anthropology, cartography, geology, climatology, botany, zoology, and history have found *Naufragios* to be a useful source of information. Much of this interest comes from efforts early in this century to trace the exact route taken by Cabeza de Vaca on his expedition.

In addition, *Naufragios*'s numerous editions and translations evidence the appeal it has to the public at large. Apparently, it held immediate interest even in its day, since a second edition appeared just thirteen years after the first. Numerous editions have followed, including five published by Espasa-Calpe alone, in this century. *Naufragios* has been translated into Italian, French, German, and English. In fact, English boasts of three complete translations, as well as a partial translation, and two paraphrased versions.[6] Spin-offs based on the narrative include several biographies, studies on Cabeza de Vaca's route, several historical novels, a canto of an epic poem, and a group of paintings.[7]

Although Covey mentions many disciplines which study *Naufragios,* he overlooks the field of literary study. Many anthologies of Spanish-American literature include portions of the work to represent the era of Discovery and Conquest. One literary historian calls the work novelesque, while others simply admire Cabeza de Vaca's narrative skill and literary power.[8]

Approximately two decades ago, the first literary studies dedicated solely to the work appeared. Perhaps predictably, most of these studies have focused on either the relationship between history and art in *Naufragios,* or artistic aspects of the work. David Lagmanovich addresses its artistic value by focusing on characteristics it shares with other works of literature.[9] Robert E. Lewis examines the relationship between history and fiction in *Naufragios* through careful analysis of the work's "Prohemio" [preface].[10] He finds that Cabeza de Vaca paid extra attention to narrative quality in the text because his journey lacked exploits considered heroic in his day. He observes that in employing novelesque techniques to describe things unknown in Europe and present himself as protagonist, Cabeza de Vaca obscures the line between history and fiction. Galeota uses a structural approach to categorize *Naufragios* as travel literature.[11] Dowling examines the work through speech-act theory, focusing on the way the work's evaluative clauses set Cabeza de Vaca up as the unerring hero of the story.[12] These critics, and others, have documented *Naufragios*'s literary triumphs, despite the fact that it is merely a chronicle of a journey.

We now turn to examination of picaresque elements in the text.

1) *Episodic Plot. Naufragios*'s overall storyline reveals an entirely episodic plot: Cabeza de Vaca departs from Spain as part of an expedition to the New World. After stops in Santo Domingo and Cuba, the expedition goes to Florida. There, most of his travel companions fall victim to the elements, and he journeys on foot for eight years until reaching Mexico City. He eventually returns to the Iberian Peninsula. A constant shift from milieu to milieu constitutes the text's most transparent episodic element. No protagonist from "classic" picaresque novels can claim to have traveled more extensively than Cabeza de Vaca. In terms both of miles traveled and variety of cultures he encounters, he far outdistances the champion traveler of picaresque novels—Guzmán de Alfarache. With just three exceptions, the people Cabeza de Vaca meets disappear forever when he renews his journey. The exceptions are his three surviving companions who also eventually return to Spain with him. However, since these men play very minor roles in the narrative, they bring no stability to Cabeza de Vaca's world. Cause-and-effect relationships do not occur between episodes. Thus, single episodes become entirely insulated, and the field of possibilities for subsequent episodes is infinite. *Naufragios*'s structure is as episodic as that of any "purely" picaresque novel.

2) *Dizzying Rhythm.* In less than 150 pages Cabeza de Vaca recounts the eight years and six thousand miles of his journey. He tells not only of the tragic events of his expedition but of his personal experiences with many native Indian tribes and his eventual return to "civilization." In a global perspective, the narrative's rhythm is vertiginous. To illustrate the rapid rhythm of the text, let us consider the action of chapters 6 and 7 (seven pages). At the outset of these chapters the expedition approaches a town. Cabeza de Vaca scouts ahead to ascertain whether the group can approach safely. Upon finding only

women and children, the expedition enters the town. Shortly thereafter the natives attack. The Spaniards take the native women and children hostage, but free them shortly thereafter. As a result, they suffer a series of attacks during the twenty-five days they spend in the area. During this period the group conducts three expeditions of reconnaissance. They depart to another town. For nine days they travel with difficulty across lagoons, rivers, and swamps. Hostile natives threaten them constantly. Upon reaching the other town Cabeza de Vaca once again undertakes a mission of reconnaissance. Two days later he returns to find his companions sick and wounded in the wake of the most brutal ambush they had encountered. In a matter of a few pages, we accompany Cabeza de Vaca for more than a month, seeing through his pen several expeditions of reconnaissance, nine days of march, and numerous altercations with the natives. In addition to the abundance of action, he manages to describe the terrain, the animals, the agricultural products, and the tactics of war. I find the rhythm as vertiginous as in any picaresque work.

3) *Fate Rules Supreme.* The whims of fate victimize Cabeza de Vaca. That the work's title changed from *Relación* to *Naufragios* evidences the protagonist's hard luck. His survival attests to good luck's role in his life. Chapters 11 and 12 provide an excellent example of the Sisyphus rhythm. At this point in the narration, the expedition has suffered two shipwrecks, numerous assaults from Indians, the loss of many men, separation from the main body of the group, and intense hunger. Cabeza de Vaca has been wounded twice in altercations with natives. In chapter 11 our hero finds himself along with eighty companions on an island after a shipwreck. Everyone suffers from cold, hunger, and physical debilitation. Suddenly, a hundred natives arrive carrying bows and arrows. Their stature intimidates the Spaniards: "agora ellos fuesen grandes o no, nuestro miedo les hacía parecer gigantes" [now whether they were large or not, our fear made them look like giants] (p. 41). This predicament could easily have led to the end of the Europeans, but fortunately the natives present their arrows to them in a token of peace. They are provided with food for many days until they recover sufficient strength to launch their crafts once again. Luck has smiled on the expedition. Nonetheless, shortly after renewing their voyage, a storm rocks them mercilessly. Now bad luck humiliates them, leaving them once again naked, hungry, and cold. Eventually

sixty-five of the eighty Spaniards who reached the island die. When they leave the island for good, the survivors, recognizing fate's hand in their lives, christen it "la isla de Mal Hado" [the island of Ill Fate] (p. 50). Fate pursues Cabeza de Vaca to the end of his journey. After his eight-year trek he arrives in Mexico City. When he finally departs for Spain, a storm destroys his ship and he must wait several more months to return. The next ship proves to be unseaworthy, and he must wait two additional weeks. He finally leaves in a three-ship flotilla, but within a few days they lose sight of the other two ships and are forced to drop anchor in Cuba for another period of time. Again he departs for Spain, but arrives only after being threatened by pirates. As with any picaresque protagonist, Cabeza de Vaca is controlled by events rather than controlling them himself. Fate plays a central role in the narrative.

4) *Bodily Violence.* Although Cabeza de Vaca does not present most of the difficulties which befall him as disgusting or grotesque, many incidents indicate that bodily violence frequently befell him and his companions. We could say that anyone who undertakes an expedition into unknown regions should expect hardships. However, sudden violent tropical storms, multiple shipwrecks, and frequent ambushes seem to be more than any one person deserves. Cabeza de Vaca surpasses most picaresque heroes in the physical punishment he suffers.

5a) *A Single Protagonist.* As with "classic" picaresque novels, Cabeza de Vaca himself unifies the text. He towers far above all secondary characters. A title such as "The Adventures of Cabeza de Vaca in North America" would reflect accurately the content of the work.

5b) *Uncommon Origins.* No mention is made of Cabeza de Vaca's origin in *Naufragios.*

5c) *Cunning.* Cabeza de Vaca shows a great capacity to adapt to the customs of the different Indian tribes he encounters. His Protean form, as outlined below, lays bare his cunning, as does his almost unbelievable ability to communicate with many tribes of Indians in spite of their different languages. At one point he claims to have learned six of the languages. When verbal communication is impossible, he manages adequate communication through gestures.

5d) *Protean Form.* As with the classic picaro, Cabeza de Vaca takes upon himself varying masks and roles in order to survive. Among several tribes he plays the part of doctor/healer (and meets with some success because some of his patients are healed—he even claims to have raised one from the dead!). On one occasion he becomes a successful business-man, functioning as a middleman in trade between tribes. In a later episode he blesses the food and children like a clergy-man. In another he promises rain, thus taking the role of rain-maker. He becomes a religious symbol to some tribes by presenting to them a certain type of gourd. He feigns anger to one tribe; by chance (once again, fate rules supreme) eight members of the tribe die shortly thereafter. As a result, the tribe fears him and gives him whatever he desires. Cabeza de Vaca changes roles with the skill of a picaro. However, I do not see evidence to indicate that such adaptability signifies interior chaos or loss of personality. Rather, I think he merely plays these parts to survive.

5e) *Alienation.* In Pedro Lastra's study, he touches on the fasci-nating issue of the "Other" in Cabeza de Vaca's writings.[13] I see his fellow Spaniards and the natives he encounters as the major "Others." As the text begins, the protagonist seems firmly bonded to his fellows. The first signs of breakdown in this relationship come when his superior officer disregards his advice and sends him on dangerous missions among the Indians. When he becomes separated from his companions, his loneliness and alienation become unbearable: "Dejo aquí de contar esto más largo, porque cada uno puede pensar lo que se pasaría en tierra tan extraña y tan mala, y tan sin ningún remedio de ninguna cosa, ni para estar ni para salir de ella" [Here I refrain from extending this account, because each reader can imagine what things were like in this land that was so strange and evil, and so lacking in any solutions, whether to stay in it or leave it] (p. 27). His constant shift from milieu to milieu does not allow him to establish any lasting relationships. In fact, he does not want to establish any. Claudio Guillén's term "half-outsider" fits Cabeza de Vaca perfectly after the first part of his narration. He adapts so well to the customs and practices of the Indians that they come to respect each other. Nevertheless, although he dresses like the Indians, speaks their language, practices their cus-toms, and admires their generosity, he remains a Spaniard and a Christian and yearns to interact with his fellow Europeans. Whereas linguistic irony dominates most picaresque novels, the greatest irony of *Naufragios* is situational. When he finally reunites with "Christians" in Northern Mexico, he finds that they treat the Indians in very un-Christian ways. The Spaniards' behavior alienates him; he remains a "half-outsider" among his own countrymen.

5f) *Internal Instability.* Cabeza de Vaca does not show signs of internal instability as do most picaros. His eight years of perseverance to arrive in Mexico City testify to his resolve. His firm religious commitment also shows stability. He attributes all successes to God and toward the end of his narrative even preaches to the Indians. The hero of *Naufragios* seems to enjoy great interior stability.

5g) *A Philosophical Bent. Naufragios* contains very few passages which reflect a philosophical bent. Any trace of philosophy is strictly Christian. The text's most extended passage dealing with Christian philosophy lasts just a few lines, during which he praises Christ for suffering much more than he on his behalf (86). Similar shorter passages are scarce; rather than wax philosophical in his writings, Cabeza de Vaca prefers to tell the events of his travels and to describe the people and places he visited.

6) *The First-person Point of View. Naufragios* indeed utilizes the first-person point of view. Although the account has a retrospective vantage point, we do not find extensive fragmentation of the narrator into a narrating self and a participating self.

7) *An Unkind, Chaotic World.* The sections above on fate and bodily violence evidence the unkind, chaotic nature of the world described by Cabeza de Vaca. Chaos reigns in that he never knows whether the next Indian tribe will be friendly or hostile, or whether the next geographical area will bring physical relief or deprivation. The world's unrelenting, unkind nature can be seen in numerous passages.

8) *Physical Survival.* Staying alive is the major recurring theme in *Naufragios.* David Lagmanovich finds in his study on *Naufragios* that the word for "hunger" occurs forty-six times in the text and that many other times the concept of hunger is conveyed through expressions such as "sin hallar otra cosa que comer" [unable to find any other thing to eat].[14] The problem of food becomes so extreme that the expedition eats its own horses. Further deprivation leads some members of the group to resort to cannibalism. In addition, references to extreme thirst, bodily exposure to the elements, assaults by Indians, and regaining strength after illness, injury, or long marches abound.

9)   *A Vast Gallery of Human Types.* Cabeza de Vaca mentions a great many types of people in *Naufragios*. However, with the possible exception of Pánfilo de Narvaez, the leader of the original expedition, emphasis rests on groups rather than individuals. In addition, little effort is expended on characterization through description and analysis; we come to know people mostly through their actions. For example, among the Spaniards, the "types" would include Narvaez, the hard-luck, hardheaded leader; the desperates, who turn to cannibalism when faced with extreme hunger; the survivors, who adapt to each situation and return to civilization, as does the narrator; and the slave-traders, who are driven by greed and treat Indians as subhuman. Types of Indian tribes include the overtly hostile and warfaring; the cunning and treacherous in military operations; the amicable who supply the Spaniards with protection and means of subsistence; the superstitious who accept Cabeza de Vaca as a "Child of the Sun"; those that accept Christian teachings; the roguish; and those that loot other Indian tribes. Never do we encounter types presented with satiric or parodic bents, such as the squire or blind man in *Lazarillo* or the schoolmaster in *El buscón*. Nonetheless, in *Naufragios* we certainly find a vast gallery of human types.

The foregoing extended analysis of picaresque elements in *Naufragios* illustrates in a concrete way the existence of a strong relationship between the picaresque and travel literature. Critics of travel literature seem most able to see this relationship, as evidenced by this statement by Sandra Rosenberg: "The particular form of fiction the travel-book most resembles is the picaresque novel."[15]

By way of contrast, most literary historians who deal with the picaresque novel seem unaware of any kinship with travel literature as they seek possible influences, attempt to outline development of the genre, or identify elements common to the picaresque and literature that precedes it. *El libro de buen amor* [*The Book of Good Love*] and *La Celestina* surface most often as probable ancestors of the picaresque.[16] Both works feature characters and themes which later became associated with the picaresque tradition. Other critics have linked the picaresque tradition to classical literature, especially to *The Golden Ass* by Lucius Apuleius. Some find similarities with other non-Spanish literatures, such as Arabic, Catalan, French, German, Portuguese, and Italian.[17]

I have found no reference in writings on the picaresque to the similarities between travel literature and the picaresque. Nonetheless, as demonstrated in the preceding pages, *Naufragios,* as a representative of travel literature, shares many elements with picaresque literature. The relationship I suggest here is not primarily thematic, as with *El libro de buen amor* and *La Celestina,* but rather structural. The episodic plot, common to travel narratives, lends itself to having just one protagonist who struggles with feelings of alienation, to showing the strength of fate, and to introducing an array of types of people.

Obviously, since *Lazarillo de Tormes*'s author is unknown, scholars cannot authoritatively pursue such influence. Notwithstanding this obstacle, speculation on the subject has been fecund and stimulating. Parallelisms between the Adam of the picaresque and works published before it certainly exist. Suggesting that *Naufragios* had an influence on *Lazarillo* would be an unpromising conjecture, although the possibility exists. Suggesting that travel literature had an influence on *Lazarillo* is a much more promising hypothesis. The fact that 1554 is the traditional date of publication given for *Lazarillo* increases the possibility of placing travel literature in the line of development of the picaresque. The narratives of the conquerors and explorers of the New World were coming to light in the first half of the sixteenth century. For example, *Naufragios,* as has been mentioned, was published in Spain in 1542. Thus, travel literature, especially with regard to structure, may have had an impact on the origins of the picaresque tradition.

Returning to the matter of *Naufragios*'s place in Mexico's literary history, perhaps its place should not be a mere forerunner of the novel, thus relegating it to a nebulous, undefined status, but a proud great uncle of *El Periquillo Sarniento.* Without question, the *Periquillo* is a direct descendant in the picaresque family. If travel literature did indeed have an influence on *Lazarillo,* then *Naufragios,* as a full-blooded member of that family, can boast of at least association with that influence. The *Periquillo* and all other heirs of the picaresque tradition in Mexico likely have *Naufragios* in their family tree. Thus, in a way heretofore unseen, *Naufragios* plays an important role in the emergence of the novel in Mexico.

3

Infortunios de Alonso Ramírez

Wherein the genre of Sigüenza y Góngora's Infortunios de Alonso Ramírez *is discussed and its picaresque qualities pointed out succinctly, after which we see how the hero of this tale of misfortunes (or at any rate, the narrator of them) elicited the sympathy of readers (implied and otherwise) by using cleverly devised stratagems that, while not necessarily evoking tearful responses, seem to have brought to the hero a greatly needed material recompense.*

CARLOS DE SIGÜENZA Y GÓNGORA'S NAME APPEARS ALONE AS the author of *Infortunios de Alonso Ramírez* [*The Misfortunes of Alonso Ramírez*], published in 1690. It originally carried an unwieldy title appropriate to the baroque tendencies of its day: *Infortunios que Alonso Ramírez, natural de la ciudad de San Juan de Puerto Rico, padeció, así en poder de ingleses piratas que lo apresaron en las Islas Filipinas como navegando por sí solo, y sin derrota, hasta varar en la costa de Yucatán: Consiguiendo por este medio dar vuelta al mundo* [*The Misfortunes that Alonso Ramírez, a Native of the City of San Juan, Puerto Rico, Suffered Both at the Hands of English Pirates who Took Him Captive in the Philippine Islands, as well as During the Time While he was Traveling Freely on the High Seas, until he Landed on the Coast of Yucatán: Accomplishing in the Process a Trip Around the World*].[1] Literary historians who seek tidy solutions to matters of authorship and generic classification find it rather bothersome. Some consider it a "relación," or travel narrative, others see in it an ancestor of the Spanish-American novel, and for others it is a full-fledged novel.

In addition to *Infortunios*'s date of publication, which disqualifies it for many from the ranks of novels, the circumstances behind its writing further complicate its generic classification. I propose that *Infortunios* can actually be considered a precursor of the most common type of modern-day autobiography. Its narrative situation shares striking similarities to the growing number of co-written autobiographies so popular today. The book *Bo,* by Bo Schembechler *and* Mitch Albom, serves as a point of comparison.[2] I use it here to represent the numerous "autobiographical" books written by celebrities with the help of more experienced writers. According to a report from newspaper columnist Bob Greene, Albom administered an extensive set of interviews to Schembechler from which he composed *Bo.*[3] Albom then made all the decisions on the sequence of material in the book, what to include or exclude, and even had freedom to touch up the transcriptions. He wrote it from a first-person, Schembechler point of view. Schembechler never actually wrote a single word of his own autobiography.

Infortunios's genesis mirrors *Bo*'s. Alonso Ramírez, believed to have been a real person, reportedly went to Sigüenza y Góngora to have the Mexican savant record his life's adventures. Since we do not have transcriptions of their encounter we obviously have no idea where the input from Ramírez ends and Sigüenza y Góngora's begins. The savant performed at least some degree of narrative transformation, for although his name appears as the text's sole author, it maintains a first-person, Ramírez point of view. If Ramírez were writing today, his name would certainly appear as a co-author of his text. In fact, to follow the modern pattern of autobiography, the size of Ramírez's name as author on the cover should cause a near eclipse of Sigüenza y Góngora's. The difference lies in the fact that in 1690, this particular writer's fame far outshone Alonso's, along with almost anyone else's in Mexico. Although Ramírez's name does not appear as author, *Infortunios* is his autobiography of sorts, just as *Bo* is Schembechler's (of sorts). Considering Ramírez's almost certain illiteracy, *Infortunios* was as close to autobiography as he could get.

On the other hand, the narrative situation parallels that of *Hasta no verte Jesús mío,* published by Elena Poniatowska in 1969.[4] Ironically, the classification of Poniatowska's book as a novel has never been questioned. *Infortunios* holds a unique place in Mexican narrative—we have either a modern "autobiography," a strikingly "novelistic" precursor of the *Periquillo,* or a novel that precedes it.

Not surprisingly, much of the critical discussion devoted to Sigüenza y Góngora's text explores the topic of its generic classification. Most literary critics tend not to consider the work a novel, but others emphatically disagree.[5] Most of the studies devoted to *Infortunios* deal with its relationship to the picaresque tradition. In each case, critics recognize its obvious ties to the subgenre, but caution against considering it a fully picaresque novel for varying reasons such as having a "non-picaresque" tone, an honest protagonist, a lack of satire, and "not being a novel."[6]

Because *Infortunios*'s picaresque nature, or lack thereof, has been discussed at length by other critics, I do so here in a very abbreviated form.

1) *Episodic Plot.* Episodes do indeed structure *Infortunios*'s plot. Alonso's extensive travels take us to numerous milieus, unified exclusively by his constant presence.

2) *Dizzying Rhythm.* Vertiginous describes the pace of the book's narration. We are whisked with the protagonist around the world and back, from situation to situation at a breakneck pace.

3) *Fate Rules Supreme.* Alonso refers more than once to his "estrella" [star], thus acknowledging luck's influence in his life. The Sisyphus rhythm characterizes several episodes.

4) *Bodily Violence.* As with *Naufragios*, this text's title testifies to the protagonist's misfortunes. As captives of pirates, Alonso and his companions experience extreme physical and psychological horrors. The pirates repeatedly threaten, beat, whip, and torture them. They force one man to eat human excrement and on another occasion serve human flesh to them. Several of Alonso's companions die as a result of the cruel treatment.

5a) *A Single Protagonist.* Alonso Ramírez is the work's only major character. All other characters are secondary.

5b) *Uncommon Origins.* Unlike the typical picaro, Alonso knows who his parents are, is not an orphan, and seems to have had a reasonably stable childhood.

5c) *Cunning.* Since our protagonist survives his ordeals he obviously has some degree of intelligence and mettle. However, his cunning is not emphasized in the text.

5d) *Protean Form.* As has been noted by other critics, Alonso serves many masters. In fact, in his short narrative, he exercises twelve professions. Although he does not don masks, his ability to change professional hats numerous times attests to his protean form.

5e) *Alienation.* Alienation never becomes the focus of *Infortunios,* even though Alonso's own relatives reject him, he never bonds completely with any person or people, and he experiences tremendous loneliness.

5f) *Internal Instability.* Unlike the typical picaro, Alonso maintains firm internal stability. His religious convictions constitute an anchor to him throughout the text.

5g) *A Philosophical Bent.* The narrator Alonso avoids philosophizing; rather, he generally narrates his life's events without editorial comment.

6) *The First-person Point of View. Infortunios* does indeed feature the autobiographical, first-person form typical of picaresque and travel narratives.

7) *An Unkind, Chaotic World.* David Lagmanovich describes the bleak world of our protagonist: "pobreza inaudita, general crueldad, inhumanas diversiones de los opresores, antropofagia, coprología; un compendio de deshumanización, contado con los colores del más descarnado realismo" [unprecedented poverty, general cruelty, inhumane actions at the hands of oppressors, cannibalism, reference to excrement; a compendium of dehumanization, narrated in the living color of the most stark realism].[7]

8) *Physical Survival.* This theme surfaces often in the text. Hunger never leaves Alonso's presence, and he also experiences intensely cold weather, thirst, and illness.

9) *A Vast Gallery of Human Types.* Although not vast or satiric, *Infortunios* does feature a number of human types, including Alonso's masters, pirates, Spanish traitors, and wife-sellers.

In the initial paragraph of *Infortunios*, the narrator states a two-fold purpose in writing: to entertain and to arouse the reader's compassion.

Sigüenza y Góngora prefaces the text with a letter to New Spain's viceroy, the implied reader of *Infortunios*. It reveals the narrator's motive in soliciting the reader's empathy. After praising the Viceroy's excellence, prudence, heritage, and generosity, Sigüenza y Góngora asks rhetorically "quién dudará el que sea [Alonso Ramírez] objeto de su munificencia en lo de adelante" [who can doubt that Alonso Ramírez will be the recipient of your munificence] (p. 32). Before closing, he calls Alonso's travels a "peregrinación lastimosa" [deplorable pilgrimage], elevating the protagonist to the level of a Saint. The letter ends with reiterative gratitude for the Viceroy's liberality. In this cover letter, Sigüenza y Góngora overtly flatters New Spain's highest government official to prepare him to find heartfelt sympathy that will extend to his pursestrings.

The work's opening paragraph contains many of the devices used extensively throughout the text to garner sympathy. Its first sentence sets the tone:

> Quiero que se entretenga el curioso que esto leyere por algunas horas con las noticias de lo que a mí me causó tribulaciones de muerte por muchos años.

[I want to entertain the curious who may read this for a few hours with tidings regarding what caused me grave tribulations for a period of many years] (p. 41).

The narrator expresses the desire to entertain, but features the emotionally packed expression "grave tribulations" to describe what he promises to narrate. In the same sentence the narrator cleverly sets up a temporal contrast between how long the reader will enjoy the text ("a few hours") and the time he spent in death's throes ("many years"). In the next sentence he contrasts his text with imaginary events, indicating that his trials are far from a fairy tale. This distinction makes a crucial difference in obtaining a sympathetic response from the reader. He marks this contrast by stating that while proverbial sayings can wrap up fictional accounts, his text defies such simplicity since his experiences are not imaginary. In the same convoluted sentence he overtly solicits sympathy:

> . . . no será esto lo que yo intente, sino solicitar lástimas que, aunque posteriores a mis trabajos, harán por lo menos tolerable su memoria. . . .

> [. . . I shall make no such attempt here, but rather I will sue for commiseration which, although it comes later than my travails, will at least make their memory tolerable. . . .] (p. 41).

He suggests that his suffering returns when merely recalling his life's events, and that his sorrow can only be mitigated by compassion from his reader. In the opening paragraph's third and final sentence, he contrasts himself with other men who would complain at length over events that have represented mere trifles for him. He warns against thinking he may have exaggerated. He expresses a disgust for faintheartedness, which seems designed to keep readers from viewing him as a whiner in spite of his pleas for sympathy. Thus, in the first paragraph of *Infortunios,* although his promise of a good story remains only a promise, the narrator's attempt to arouse the reader's compassion has already begun. In fact, despite the purposes declared in the paragraph's initial sentence, the narrator spends much more time and effort in the opening paragraph arousing sympathy than entertaining.

The foregoing sympathy-eliciting tactics surface throughout the text. Perhaps the book's most effective stratagem is contrast or counterpoint, a prominent technique in Baroque art. The Sisyphus rhythm, a device often mentioned as typical of picaresque texts, constitutes a major use of contrast in the first half of *Infortunios*. Upon obtaining his first employment, Alonso experiences a new sensation of being in control of his life enough to stop worrying about his next meal. His stability is threatened when a deathly illness grips his master, but Alonso manages to nurse him back to health. With his future seemingly secure, his master suddenly dies. The emotional impact of Alonso's plight intensifies because he appeared to be on the verge of perpetual prosperity.

Some time thereafter Alonso manages to marry into an honorable, established, affluent family. This again seems to render secure his financial position. Not only does he enjoy economic steadiness, but his wife nurtures him with love, providing him emotional security. Nonetheless, she dies in childbirth within a year of their marriage. The family irrevocably severs ties from Alonso. His return to rootlessness seems worse because it follows the promise of stability.

The Sisyphus rhythm jolts Alonso and his readers most violently in an episode set near the Philippines. His diligence as a seafaring merchant eventually leads him to become the commander of a ship and its crew of twenty-five men. His outlook on life reaches a zenith. However, on his first voyage as commander, his ship and crew fall captive to ruthless pirates. Once again, the tragedy carries deeper emotional impact because it contrasts with a hard-earned moment of great promise.

The narrator skillfully uses another type of contrast as a counterpoint to his travails by presenting various settings as strikingly attractive. The first such passage describes his homeland, Puerto Rico:

> Hácenla célebre los refrescos que hallan en su deleitosa aguada cuantos desde la antigua navegan sedientos a la Nueva España; la hermosura de su bahía, lo incontrastable del Morro que la defiende; las cortinas y baluartes coronados de artillería que la aseguran.

> [The refreshment found in its delightful water supply by those who sail, suffering great thirst, from old to New Spain; the beauty of its bay, the overwhelming strength of the "Morro" fortress which defends it; the curtains and bulwarks crowned by the artillery which protect it] (p. 42).

After painting a beautiful picture of Puerto Rico, he explains that hard times came to the island and caused poverty among its inhabitants. Thus, at the age of thirteen he was cast out of his homeland into the cruel world. The pain of his adult purgatory intensifies through its contrast with a sheltered childhood paradise, secured by the physical stronghold "El Morro."

Alonso's capture and subsequent nightmarish interval as a prisoner of the pirates contrasts not only with his former economic stability, but with the beauty of Manila:

> Hállase allí para el sustento y vestuario cuanto se quiere a moderado precio. . . . Esto, y lo hermoso y fortalecido de la ciudad, coadyuvado con la amenidad de su río y huertas, y lo demás que la hace célebre entre las colonias que tienen los europeos en el Oriente, obliga a pasar gustosos a los que en ella viven.

> [One can find there as much sustenance and clothing as a person could want at reasonable prices. . . . This, and the city's beauty and security, along with the amenity of its river and orchards, and all the things which make it famous above all the colonies which Europe holds in the East, force all who live there to enjoy it] (p. 54).

Alonso's frequent reference to a site's defenses reveals his yearning for stability. Once again, his plight seems more pitiable because it contrasts with beautiful, and secure, surroundings.

The structure of *Infortunios* works to arouse the reader's compassion. The length of each of the text's seven sections reveals an emphasis on key elements of the narrator's life. The first recounts Alonso's childhood and struggles in many towns and with numerous masters in Mexico. The second section gives nautical information for the trip Alonso takes from Acapulco to the Philippines, tells of the places he visits after arriving in the Orient, and relates his capture by pirates. Part three describes Alonso's agonizing experiences as a captive of the pirates. Part four briefly informs of his release from the buccaneers, but reflects at length on the captivity. In part five Alonso and his company sail to the Caribbean, where a tropical storm destroys their ship. Section six relates Alonso's heroism in helping his companions reach shore safely, and their expedition northward in the Yucatán peninsula. In the final section Alonso and his men travel to a number of Mexican cities, telling their story as they go. In this section Alonso eventually tells his story to the Viceroy and Sigüenza y Góngora.

In the Cordillera edition of the text, the length of each section is as follows:

Section	Number of Pages
I	9
II	8
III	15
IV	10
V	8
VI	10
VII	12

Section three, the text's longest, recounts the atrocities committed by pirates on Alonso's ship. He allows himself extra opportunity to tell added details of the most harrowing experiences of his life.

Section four begins with Alonso's final, and most life-threatening experience with the pirates. His captors finally decide that their captives hold no value for them. They meet in council to decide their victims' fate. The discussion as to whether to free Alonso and his men or kill them becomes so heated that the pirates almost come to blows among themselves. At this moment, the narrator overtly seeks the empathy of his reader: "póngase en mi lugar quien aquí llegare y discurra de qué tamaño sería el susto y la congoja con que yo estuve" [to whomever arrives at this point and ponders how great the fright and pain was that I felt, put yourself into my place] (p. 76). The narrator could not have found a more effective moment for such a plea. If the reader heeds his advice, sympathy for the protagonist seems inevitable.

In contrast with the chronological order that marks every other chapter, section four suspends the chronology. Verbal tense reflects this contrast. During most of the text, the preterit dominates, as the narrator moves swiftly from event to event. However, in section four the narrator pauses, using the imperfect tense to look retrospectively at the awful conditions of his captivity. Thus, Alonso's nightmarish experiences with the pirates not only receive full account in the longest section of the book, but their horror extends in the subsequent section through departure from the narrative's verbal and chronological norms.

The adventures described in the text's final section pale compared to the horror of captivity by the pirates; nonetheless, they comprise the text's second-longest section. The narrator creates ample opportunity to show that his suffering continues into the present. This brings immediacy to his pleas for sympathy and financial relief. Thus, although *Infortunios* has a simple, episodic structure, the narrator astutely exploits its possibilities.

David Lagmanovich calls the tone of *Infortunios* "tremendista," even though the term was coined in reference to twentieth-century literature.[8] The following represents one such passage:

> . . . metiéronme a mí y a los míos en la bodega, desde donde percibí grandes voces y un trabucazo; pasado un rato y habiéndome hecho salir afuera, vide mucha sangre, y mostrándomela, dijeron ser de uno de los míos a quien habían muerto, y que lo mismo sería de mí si no respondía a propósito de lo que me preguntaban . . .

> [. . . they placed me and my men into the supply room, from which I heard loud voices and a musket shot; some time later they took me outside where I saw a profusion of blood; as they showed it to me, they said that it was from one of my men whom they had killed, and that I would meet the same fate if I didn't answer directly their questions . . .] (p. 61).

The narrator does not save his reader from the sight of blood or horror. However, rather than expounding on violent and shocking scenes, he glides past them without great ado, communicating the impression that he has suffered so greatly that events that shock us are commonplace to him. Other "tremendista" passages narrate in a very matter-of-fact tone how a man's hands were severed, the violent whippings they endured, and acts of cannibalism. With the exception of the passage describing the pirates' cannibalism, the narrator never intervenes with his personal reaction to graphically violent events. The emotional gap between the reader's shock and the narrator's indifference inspires further pathos.

A final strategy that arouses the reader's sympathy centers on the character of the protagonist. Several critics disqualify Alonso as a picaro because he is far too responsible. He not only works hard to serve his masters, but never fails them in loyalty. Furthermore, rather than hold a cynical outlook on his fellow beings, he liberally praises those he finds worthy of commendation. These details regarding the character of our protagonist help him to gain the reader's compassion. Alonso's trials have not been self-imposed through personal caprice; instead, fate has dealt him heavy blows. The first word of the text's title indicates this rather forcefully. As a victim of tremendously extenuating circumstances rather than of his own doing, he earns our pity more freely.

We do not depend entirely on critical opinion to judge whether Alonso and/or Sigüenza y Góngora, meet the goals of their "autobiography." In the third to last paragraph of the text, Alonso tells of visiting Sigüenza y Góngora to recount his life story. The ensuing passage indicates the fruits of their encounter:

> Compadecido [Sigüenza] de mis trabajos, no sólo formó esta Relación en que se contienen, sino que me consiguió con la intercesión y súplicas que en mi presencia hizo al Excmo. Sr. Virrey, Decreto para que D. Sebastián de Guzmán y Córdoba, factor veedor y proveedor de las cajas reales me socorriese, como se hizo.

> [Having sympathy for my travails, (Sigüenza) not only wrote this account that contains them, but also arranged for an audience with and petitioned on my behalf before his most Excellent Viceroy, for a decree that Don Sebastián de Guzmán y Córdoba, purveyor of the royal treasury, come to my aid, which did indeed occur] (p. 114).

Modern autobiographies are often judged by their financial success. These comments, apparently added to the text after the Viceroy received it, indicate that Alonso Ramírez achieved success even by today's standards. Not only did he arouse compassion in Sigüenza y Góngora, but he did the same with the text's implied reader, the Viceroy. Probably of infinitely greater importance to Alonso, the latter translated into financial reward. This postlude signals an "autobiographical" triumph—Alonso not only accomplished his two-pronged aim to entertain the reader and arouse his compassion, but he can claim success in the modern-day bottom line of financial increase.

4

El Periquillo Sarniento

Wherein note is made of the historical importance of the renowned symbol of the emergence of the novel in Spanish America, El Periquillo Sarniento, *its picaresque elements examined, and the artistry of its secondary character portrayal studied, with particular attention paid to the masterful depiction of Celidonio Matamoros, alias Dr. Purgante.*

AMONG THE BEST-KNOWN DATES IN MEXICO AND SPANISH America's literary history is the publication year of *El Periquillo Sarniento,* José Joaquín Fernández de Lizardi's masterpiece.[1] Because of the *Periquillo*'s appearance in 1816, most literary historians consider it the debut year of the novel in Mexico and Spanish America. By far the most renowned of Mexico's picaresque narratives, the *Periquillo*'s literary significance looms even larger in the scope of this study. It serves as the literary point of reference for all other texts referred to herein. We need not explain its context; instead, it creates context.[2]

Since the *Periquillo* is a well-known and complex work, it has received considerable critical attention.[3] Jefferson Rea Spell has done the most extensive work on Fernández de Lizardi and his literary production. In fact, his dissertation, entitled "The Life and Works of José Joaquín Fernández de Lizardi," was "the first work based on a Mexican writer offered to the academic English-speaking world."[4] In it, *Bridging The Gap,* and many additional articles, Spell not only gives considerable information about El Pensador Mexicano's life, but tells of the *Periquillo*'s genesis, its sociohistorical background, its possible sources, and differences among its first four editions. Spell states that Lizardi holds a unique place in Mexican literature:

He created the first Mexican novel; he brought that form of fiction down to the level of the common people; he linked the Mexican novel in peculiar fashion with that of a typical form of Spanish literature; in his attention to realistic detail and color, he was a forerunner of the

47

costumbristas; and he turned the attention of later Mexican writers to the fascinating material offered by the colorful life about them.[5]

Critics continue to find *El Periquillo Sarniento* worthy of their attention. For example, a recent article by Nancy Vogeley compares Lizardi to twentieth-century writers such as Carlos Fuentes, Julio Cortázar, and Guillermo Cabrera Infante in that they have all "attacked the pomposity and pretense of inherited literary taste and relied heavily on overlooked indigenous speech styles to create a hybrid product."[6] She points out that many voices from Colonial Mexico are heard in the text, whether represented directly or parroted through Periquillo's speech, even though at times in a parodic context. According to Vogeley, the *Periquillo* portrays, and symbolically reconciles, many of the diverse elements of Colonial Mexico.

Let us now turn to an examination of the work's picaresque elements.

1) *Episodic Plot.* The *Periquillo*'s plot structure is not as purely episodic as the ideal picaresque model. It falls short in that Periquillo is not the only link among all the episodes. Several secondary characters appear in more than one episode, especially in the first and last sections of the book. For example, Januario, better known by his nickname of Juan Largo, appears in an episode that takes place at a school, then later in another that takes place at a hacienda, then in a series of episodes in which he and Periquillo work together as gambling partners, and finally as a thief. In fact, many of the characters whom Periquillo meets during the course of his life appear again in the book's final episodes. In spite of the foregoing, the overall structure of the book is indeed episodic, and Periquillo is the only major link from beginning to end. Thus, although not absolutely episodic in the pure picaresque sense, the *Periquillo* remains effectively episodic.

2) *Dizzying Rhythm.* The overall narrative pace of the *Periquillo* is definitely not dizzying. As is well known, the bulk of the book's more than four hundred pages consists of digressions that do not take the story forward at all. In the first chapter, following in the literary footsteps of Guzmán de Alfarache, the narrator even warns his readers of the digressive nature of the text (p. 13). Even though short portions of the text feature rapid transitions between Periquillo's adventures,

most notably during the book's second portion, these sections are insignificant compared to the turtle's pace of the majority of the text.

3) *Fate Rules Supreme.* With some regularity, the narrator speaks of "la fortuna" [fortune] or uses the expression "quiso Dios" [God willed]. Such expressions indicate that the narrator/protagonist at least perceives that he is not in complete control of his life, but rather is victim to the whims of fate or a higher being. An anthologized incident from Periquillo's life, the episode in which he works as a pharmacist's apprentice, illustrates the role of luck in his life. He causes the death of a man when, due to hard luck, he unintentionally gives the man arsenic instead of the drug he thought he was providing. Furthermore, Periquillo's uncanny reunions with a great many of his former acquaintances, toward the book's end, provide added evidence of fate's hand. Although not a high-profile motif throughout the text, luck plays a significant role in Periquillo's life.

4) *Bodily Violence.* On occasion Periquillo is the victim of physical abuse; likewise, he occasionally metes out physical injury as well. Examples of the former include an unfortunate experience when he is victimized by a bull in a bullfight, a beating by a mother who suspects him of advances toward her daughter, and a thrashing at the hands of losing gambling opponents. An example of Periquillo causing injury is the episode in which he inflicts unbelievable pain on a woman with a toothache while serving as apprentice to a *barbero* [barber/bloodletter]. Thus, bodily violence is indeed a theme in the *Periquillo.*

5a) *A Single Protagonist.* Pedro Sarmiento, better known by his nickname of Periquillo Sarniento, is the work's only possible protagonist. All other characters in the book are clearly secondary.

5b) *Uncommon Origins.* Periquillo is a son in a middle-class family. Both his parents are alive during the early part of his life, although he perceives that their role in his upbringing was too minor. His mother spoils him by never disciplining him, and his father's good intentions for discipline are foiled because he defers to his wife. His father and then his mother die, thus, like the classic picaro, he is an orphan throughout most of the book. However, his parents' deaths come after they have provided him schooling and opportunities to continue in a middle-class situation. Although his origins are not ideal, Periquillo seems to represent an ordinary member of Colonial Mexico's middle class.

5c) *Cunning*. As a small child, Periquillo is seen to develop a capacity for manipulation when he finds that by crying, his mother grants him any whim. On numerous occasions we see that he has a talent for falsifying and deceiving to benefit himself. At one point he even boasts: "cuando yo quería era capaz de engañar al demonio" [when I so desired, I was capable of cheating the devil] (p. 231).

5d) *Protean Form*. Of the picaros examined in this study, Periquillo excels in this category. The list of professions he practices includes scribe, friar, student, beggar, thief, storekeeper, writer, go-between, and servant or apprentice to many masters. In addition, clothes obsess Periquillo, and by virtue of the fact that he buys new clothing as often as he can afford it, his physical appearance is always changing. Furthermore, he often and accurately uses the verb "fingir" to describe his interpersonal relationships. For example, he feigns cowardice to a band of thieves to avoid participating in their raids. Thus, Periquillo's form, in his physical appearance, his actions, and his self-portrayal, constantly changes.

5e) *Alienation*. Incredibly, in spite of Periquillo's disloyalty and unworthiness, several characters in the book treat him with unconditional friendship. However, until his repentance and reformation, he abuses the trust and charity of these friends and everyone he meets, thus thrusting himself into a realm of alienation. In fact, during most of the book, Periquillo surrounds himself with "friends" equally lacking in loyalty and human concern for others. Toward the end of the book he describes his state as: "despreciado de mis amigos y abandonado de todo el mundo" [despised by my friends and abandoned by the entire world] (p. 403). However, following his repentance, his capacity to love and accept love increase dramatically, and he dies surrounded by loved ones.

5f) *Internal Instability*. Early in the book we see Periquillo spending his school time arguing with the teacher for the mere sake of arguing rather than learning. This sets the stage for his lifetime of internal unsteadiness. He has a weakness for women and gambling, and never holds down a job. The novel repeatedly preaches that people need to train for a profession; Periquillo's shortcomings in this aspect lay bare his internal instability in a most prominent way.

5g) *A Philosophical Bent*. Early in the book Periquillo states: "voy escribiendo mi vida según me acuerdo, y adornándola con los consejos, crítica y erudición que puedo" [I am proceeding to write the story of my life as I recall it, and decorate it with the advice, criticism, and scholarship as I am able] (p. 41). True to his word, Periquillo manages to adorn the history of his life with generous helpings of philosophizing. Critics recognize that Lizardi wrote the novel primarily to express his views on a variety of subjects, and although most have pointed to its sermonizing passages as its weakness, some critics, among them Nancy Vogeley, see them as an artistic and informational strength.

6) *The First-person Point of View.* The narrative situation of the *Periquillo* conforms to the classic picaresque model in that it uses the first-person, retrospective perspective to narrate the picaro's life events and present tense when philosophizing. However, rather than addressing himself to a *Señor,* the narrator instead speaks to his children.

7) *An Unkind, Chaotic World.* Periquillo finds himself in numerous settings that are nothing short of revolting. Others give less offense, but the novel's overall depiction of late colonial Mexican society portrays it as far less than ideal. Periquillo's trip to the Orient provides a stark contrast to Mexico and its society. Whereas order and industry reign in the Orient, chaos, indolence, and incompetence dominate Mexico. Thieves, swindlers, and quacks make Mexican society not only chaotic, but dangerous as well.

8) *Physical Survival.* Hunger is Periquillo's most constant companion throughout the book. The following is perhaps the most eloquent expression of one of his periods of physical need:

> Desnudo y muerto de hambre sufrí algunos cuantos meses más de prisión . . . estaba demasiado pálido y flaco, y con sobrada causa, porque yo comía mal y poco, y los piojos bien y bastante.

> [Naked and starving to death, I endured several more months of prison . . . I was too pale and gaunt, and with good reason, because I ate rarely and poorly, and the lice ate often and well] (p. 205).

Sickness, exposure, fatigue, and hunger constantly populate the stage of Periquillo's drama.

9) *A Vast Gallery of Human Types. El Periquillo Sarniento* features a long, rich, and varied parade of human types. It begins

with foolish parents, continues with different types of school-teachers, and then with a wise vicar, an unfaithful friend, *léperos* [a Mexican term for course, ill-mannered individuals), convicted felons, quack doctors, Indians, a military man, beggars, and so forth. Indeed, the *Periquillo* features a vast and outstanding gallery of character types.

Given the length of the *Periquillo,* it should come as no surprise that it features a long list of secondary characters. Of more importance, the group of characters Periquillo meets distinguishes itself more in its variety of types than in its sheer length. For example, we meet not just one schoolteacher type, but three: one whose mental capacity should have disqualified him for the work; one who, though intelligent, deals so strictly and severely with his students as to make learning nearly impossible; and finally, one who combines intelligence, love for his students, and common sense to create an environment of learning. Nonetheless, even though it offers a gallery of secondary characters both extensive and varied, its greatest merit lies in the brilliant portrayal of many of these characters, even though the picaresque structure of the text prevents rounded, complete portraits. Despite their brief existence, many of them have remarkable resonance. We now examine some of the techniques employed by the author to create vivid, memorable characters.

A certain Dr. Purgante constitutes one of the novel's most enduring secondary characters. As is often the case with memorable characters, this one begins with a memorable name. The first mention of Dr. Purgante in the text dwells on his name: "Había en aquella época en esta capital un médico viejo a quien llamaban por mal nombre el doctor Purgante, porque a todos los enfermos decía que facilitaba la curación con un purgante" [At that time in this capital city there was an old physician who people mischievously called Dr. Purgante because he told all his patients that taking a laxative would help in their healing] [purgante = laxative] (p. 231). The fact that he has a nickname at all alerts us immediately to the fact that his reputation does not sparkle. Although the text provides an explanation of the nickname's origin, its implications continue with us each time we see it in the text. Even though he claims to be purging the sick of their illnesses, his reliance on laxatives has a grotesque, opposite effect; instead, he proves more effective at purging the world of people and cleansing his patients of good humor and health. Dr. Purgante's real name complements the humorous suggestions of his nickname because it not only smacks of pretensions, it adapts nicely to describing his practice of medicine: "en realidad se llamaba don Celidonio Matamoros; aunque con más verdad podía haberse llamado *Matacristianos*" [his name was actually Celidonio Matamoros (literally "moor killer"); although he could more truthfully have been called *Matacristianos* ("Christian killer")] (p. 263).

Rapid sketch, verbal caricature characterizes the method used to describe Dr. Purgante's physical appearance:

Era este sujeto alto, flaco de cara y piernas, y abultado de panza, trigueño y muy cejudo, ojos verdes, nariz de caballete, boca grande y despoblada de dientes, calvo, por cuya razón usaba en la calle peluquín con bucles.

[He was tall, thin through his face and legs, had a bulging gut, olive-skin, bushy eyebrows, green eyes, a trestle nose, a large mouth emptied of all its teeth, and was bald, because of which he wore a wig with curls when he left his house] (p. 235).

This description evokes that of a comic-strip figure, since all the characteristics described have an entirely visual orientation and emphasize bold, humorous attributes. Absence and abundance in the description create an especially effective counterpoint: his elongated, frail legs and face contrast with a hefty midsection; his absence of hair diverges markedly from both his thick eyebrows and ridiculous wig; and finally his large but toothless mouth provides stark counterpoint with his considerable nose. Dr. Purgante's ridiculous attire adds flavor to his caricatured physical appearance. When the doctor meets with Periquillo to propose that he become his servant, he wears a full-length, flowered robe, and a large, stiff, shiny beret. When he performs his medical "duties," he carefully dons an oversized ruffled collar. Thus, Dr. Purgante's grotesque physical appearance constitutes an important element in his memorable portrayal.

Dr. Purgante's flamboyant manner of speech creates the idea of caricature as effectively as his physical appearance. His first words in the novel provide an excellent case in point: "¡Oh, Periquillo, hijo! ¿Por qué extraños horizontes has venido a visitar este tugurio?" [Oh, Periquillo, my boy! Through what strange horizons have you come to visit this slum?] (p. 235). We see immediately that his speech has a dramatic flair combined with a penchant for unnatural, pedantic expressions. His frequent use of Latin further illustrates his propensity for obscure language: "En esta *domo* tendrás *in primis* el *panem nostrum quotidianum; aliunde,* lo potable necesario; *tertio,* la cama *sic vel sic* . . . " [In this *domo* you will have *in primis* the *panem nostrum quotidianum; aliunde,* all that is necessary to drink; *tertio,* a bed *sin vel sic*] (p. 236). Of course, utilization of such terms makes communication virtually impossible.

Dr. Purgante's manner of speech merely functions as a smokescreen to hide his medical incompetence, in which his ignorance is exceeded only by his vanity. His complete confidence in Periquillo, who manipulates him mercilessly by means of boundless, insincere, unfounded praise, provides undeniable evidence of his vanity.

By virtue of his ignorance and apathy in exercising his profession, he discounts human suffering and exploits it for his personal gain, revealing an absolute lack of concern for others. He and Nicolás, the pharmacist, highly recommend each other to their clients in spite of having full knowledge of their mutual incompetence. He proves to be incapable of loyalty, evidenced when he ends business ties with Nicolás, in spite of their economic interdependence, for increased income through Periquillo and an in-house pharmacy.

Curiously, we never see concrete encounters between Dr. Purgante and his patients. Nor do we have word of specific prescriptions or medical recommendations he makes. Instead, we see his work mirrored in Periquillo. The crowning touch of Dr. Purgante's portrayal comes when Periquillo steals his medical garb, literature, learning, speech, and methods, and continues his characterization in his absence. Thus, although we never see Dr. Purgante personally at work, we see him through Periquillo, who uses large doses of Latin and luck to establish a medical practice in Tula. He vividly describes his method as he works with a dying man in the presence of his grieving family:

Inmediatamente me acerqué a la cama, le tomé el pulso, miré a las vigas del techo por largo rato, después le tomé otro pulso haciendo mil monerías, como eran arquear las cejas, arrugar la nariz, mirar al suelo, morderme los labios, mover la cabeza a uno y otro lado y hacer cuantas mudanzas pantomímicas me parecieron oportunas . . .

[I immediately drew near the bed, took his pulse, looked at the beams on the ceiling for a long while, then took his pulse again, clowning around in a thousand ways, like raising my eyebrows, wrinkling up my nose, looking at the floor, biting my lips, moving my head from side to side and doing as many pantomimic gestures as came to my head] (p. 243).

Finally, when the man nears death and a priest begins to perform last rites, Periquillo orders his assistant, Andrés, to perform a major bloodletting. Miraculously, the patient improves immediately, and Periquillo accepts a handsome sum of money.

In summary, the following techniques make Dr. Purgante an unforgettable character. First, he has a humorous name and an equally catchy nickname. Second, he has a flamboyant, caricaturesque physical appearance. Third, his speech combines humorous pedantry and pathetic lack of concern for his fellow beings. This combination lays bare the huge discrepancy between the high principles of his profession and the greedy, unfeeling way in which he works. Last, his overly dramatic actions, brilliantly mirrored through Periquillo, conceal his medical incompetence. Dr. Purgante does not come across as a rounded, well-developed character, but the foregoing methods of characterization come together to create a brilliant, memorable type.

Many other secondary characters in the novel burst to life through the same techniques which created Dr. Purgante. For example, numerous characters have memorable names. Agustín Rapamentas seems a natural name for a barber [rapar = to shave]. Periquillo's first master, Cosme Casalla is better known as Chanfaina [Shambles], which Periquillo finds apt on two counts: "ya por la asonancia de esta palabra con su apellido, o ya por lo que sabía revolver" [for the rhyme it made with his surname, or for the fact that he knew how to stir things up] (p. 211). Don Severo Justiniano's [reminiscent of "Severe" or "Strict Justice"] name fits the novel's attorney most appropriately. Juan Largo [Juan Long] is the nickname of Periquillo's tall friend who, as the name suggests, keeps him in trouble for a long time. A thief Periquillo meets in jail sports the nickname Aguilita [Little Eagle] because of his quick wit and sharp claw. Many characters are best known by their character type, as in *El juicioso vicario* [The Wise Vicar], *El profesor tonto* [The Witless Teacher], *El indio macero* [The Mace-bearing Indian], *El subdelegado* [The Administrator], *El egoísta* [The Egoist], and *El misántropo* [The Misanthrope]. In most of these cases, the narrator mentions no name or nickname; even when one exists, a type best identifies the subject. In any event, many of the characters in the text attain instant recognizability by virtue of a conspicuously symbolic or humorous given name, nickname, or type name.

Verbal caricature of physical attributes delineates the portrayal of many characters in the text. For example, "gordo, aplastado, chato, cabezón, encuerado y demasiadamente vivo y atrevido" [fat, smashed-down, big-nosed, big-headed, naked and too lively and daring] describes Aguilita (p. 195). The physical description of Periquillo's strict teacher moves rapidly into a description of his personality: "Era alto, seco, entrecano, bastante bilioso e hipocondríaco, hombre de bien a toda prueba, arrogante lector . . ." [He was tall, dry, graying, rather bilious and hyphchondriacal, a good man by all accounts, an arrogant reader] (p. 23). At times very few penstrokes create a physical description which translates into a mental picture, as with Juan Largo: "Era de un cuerpo gallardo, alto y bien formado" [He had a striking body, tall and well proportioned] (p. 44). Thus, use of rapid, vivid description of physical attributes is an effective tool of characterization in the text.

Nancy Vogeley mentions that in the course of the novel many different character types have voice either directly or through Periquillo. We have seen such a case with Dr. Purgante. The *léperos* whom Periquillo meets likewise take form through speech characterization. The terms they use differ so greatly from standard Spanish that when they speak to him, he cannot understand them without an explanation from Juan Largo. After telling Periquillo that they have their own dialect, Juan Largo expounds on the meanings of many of their expressions, beginning with the following: "Por ahora sábete que *hacer la mañana* entre esta gente quiere decir desayunarse con aguardiente . . ." [Be informed that *doing the morning* among these people means to eat breakfast with liquor] (p. 136). Scribes and lawyers use ridiculous legal jargon, foreigners and Indians have at least some accent, and a more full study of differing dialects in the book would undoubtedly yield fascinating results. In any event, speech represents one of the *Periquillo*'s most effective tools of character portrayal.

Finally, some characters stand out principally due to their actions. Juan Largo's cruel practical jokes with which he victimizes Periquillo distinguish him. Antonio Sánchez makes his mark when, out of the kindness of his heart, he brings food and encouragement to Periquillo in jail. Although he appears in a variety of episodes, Andrés stands out primarily for his antics as Periquillo's medical sidekick, when he dupes an entire town into believing that the protagonist has excellent medical skills. Indeed, many characters in the *Periquillo* become memorable mainly by performing a memorable role, even in just one episode.

We have examined the skillful and extensive use of four techniques for character portrayal in Lizardi's masterpiece. Whereas all four techniques combine to create Dr. Purgante, most of the novel's secondary characters exist by virtue of skillful use of only one or two of the tactics. The episodic narrative structure of picaresque novels makes the creation of memorable characters a very difficult task. The gallery of lively, varied, memorable secondary characters in the *Periquillo,* one of its truly outstanding characteristics, attests to the fact that Lizardi rose to the task. Skillful use of the techniques of character portrayal analyzed in this study constitute a major reason for much of the enduring charm of *El Periquillo Sarniento.*

5

Don Catrín de la Fachenda

Wherein the invisibility, but not inferiority, complex suffered by Fernández de Lizardi's Don Catrín de la Fachenda *is noted and its picaresque elements set forth, after which we see how, through skillful creation of a bombastically pretentious first-person narrator though whom irony is created and sustained throughout the text, the author examines many foibles of early nineteenth-century Mexican society without subjecting readers to dreary didacticism, instead treating them to a highly entertaining work of art.*

VIDA Y HECHOS DEL FAMOSO CABALLERO DON CATRÍN DE LA *Fachenda* [*The Life and Works of the Famous Gentleman Mr. Dandy Conceited*] written in 1820 by José Joaquín Fernández de Lizardi and published posthumously in 1832, is the overlooked little brother of *El Periquillo Sarniento* (1816).[1] The *Periquillo* is better known primarily because it happened to be written and published before *Don Catrín.* The *Periquillo*'s place in many literary histories as the first Spanish-American novel has made it the star of Lizardi's literary family. Its fame has guaranteed that the names of Lizardi's other novelistic works will always be remembered; however, their automatic association with the *Periquillo* also seems to doom them. Lizardi's best-known work shines in anthologies, but is practically inaccessible as a work on its own. Its didactic nature combined with its sheer length make a complete reading unattractive to all but masochists and specialists. These attributes make study of Lizardi's other works seem equally unattractive. *La Quijotita y su prima* [*Quijotita and her Cousin*] and *Noches tristes y día alegre* [*Sad Nights and Cheerful Day*] (1818), Lizardi's other novelistic efforts, have also contributed to *Don Catrín*'s oblivion. Although both works differ greatly in style and content from the *Periquillo,* neither has received particularly favorable critical attention. *Don Catrín,* therefore, as a member of a family distinguished more by chronology than by literary merit, has nearly been forgotten.

Very few critical writings have focused on Lizardi's last novel.

Discussion of *Don Catrín* has occurred almost exclusively in literary histories and anthology introductions, always riding on the *Periquillo*'s coattails. For example, Angel Flores mentions *Don Catrín* and *La Quijotita* at the end of his introductory paragraph on Lizardi before introducing an anthology piece from *Periquillo*. He lumps them together by saying that the later novels have the same moralizing voice and satire as the earlier novel, but that their plot lacks the *Periquillo*'s interest.[2] John E. Englekirk et al. mention it along with *La Quijotita* as showing "the same didactic criticism of morals as the *Periquillo*."[3] Such statements mislead readers into believing that all three novels are basically similar. Later, Enrique Anderson-Imbert recognized the stark differences between *Don Catrín* and its famous literary sibling. Although he mentions it on the heels of *Periquillo,* Anderson-Imbert considers it Lizardi's masterpiece. Among its advantages over *Periquillo,* he mentions that it avoids lengthy digressions, the action moves smoothly and rapidly, the episodes consistently entertain, and it features skillfully used irony.[4] Fernando Alegría judges *Don Catrín* as Lizardi's novel most likely to satisfy modern critics. He compliments Catrín's psychology and the narrative technique of transferring the narrative voice from the protagonist to his assistant in the novel's final chapter.[5] John Brushwood focuses on the protagonist of *Don Catrín,* observing that he differs greatly from the *Periquillo*'s picaro because Catrín satirizes the "dandy" of his day.[6]

Jefferson Rea Spell wrote earliest and most prolifically about Lizardi. However, most of his research and writings deal with Lizardi as a person and with *El Periquillo Sarniento.* His 1931 book on Lizardi contains little more than a paragraph of comments on *Don Catrín.* This paragraph merely summarizes some of the highlights of the protagonist's life.[7] Despite editing and writing introductions to three editions of *Don Catrín,* his comments about the work are minimal. In the 1959 edition, Spell does venture to say that it exhibits the most technical artistry of Lizardi's novels.[8]

Almost all of the few critical articles that deal with *Don Catrín* do so in comparison with one or more of Lizardi's other novels. The following pair of titles show how it has not escaped association with the *Periquillo:* "The *Periquillo Sarniento* and *Don Catrín de la Fachenda:* which is the masterpiece?" and "*Periquillo* and *Catrín:* comparison and contrast."[9] Even Paul Borgeson, Jr.'s study on the narrative techniques in *Don Catrín* and *Noches tristes* refers constantly to the *Periquillo* as a point of comparison.[10] María Casas de Faunce's book gives a detailed summary of *Don Catrín,* but offers minimal critical observations.[11]

In summary, despite *Don Catrín*'s noble heritage, at the time of this writing it has received little substantive critical discussion. The highly favorable judgments expressed by most of its critics make this situation especially peculiar. Critical neglect has plagued Lizardi's last, and perhaps finest, novel.

Let us now turn to the examination of *Don Catrín de la Fachenda*'s picaresque qualities.

1) *Episodic Plot.* More than twenty-five episodes fill *Don Catrín*'s fourteen brief chapters. Several episodes interconnect with another in some way. For example, the episode that ends with the amputation of Catrín's leg provides much of the "cause" for the subsequent episode, in which he begs alms to survive. However, we find minimal cause-effect relationships between episodes, and see most of the characters and locales insulated from other episodes. The following chart illustrates the relative episodic nature of the different parts of the book:

Chapter Number	Number of Characters Other than Catrín in the Chapter	Number of These Characters that Reappear in Other Chapters	Number of Episodes in the Chapter
I	2	2	1
II	3	2	2
III	5	5	1
IV	3	3	2
V	4	2	3
VI	5	2	2
VII	4	1	2
VIII	2	0	1
IX	3	0	2
X	6	0	5
XI	3	1	3
XII	4	2	3
XIII	2	1	1
XIV	3	1	1

Of the thirty-four characters that interact with the protagonist, only seven appear in more than one chapter. These statistics prove the novel highly, though not purely, episodic.

2) *Dizzying Rhythm.* Chapters four through twelve feature episodes that occur at a truly hectic pace. Their twenty-two epi-

sodes take place in just sixty-nine pages. The following represents one of the novel's most brisk episodes:

> Hallé un monigote alquilón que se compadeció de mí y me llevó a su casa. Allí estuve algunos días. Tenía una hermana bonita; me gustó, la enamoré, condescendió, fuimos amigos; el monigote lo supo, nos espió, nos cogió y me dio tal tarea de trancazos, que volví a visitar el hospital.

> [I met a fool landlord who had pity on me and took me to his home. I was there for a few days. He had a pretty sister; I liked her, wooed her, she acquiesced, we became friends; the fool found out, spied on us, caught us, and gave me such a beating that I went back to the hospital] (p. 81).

In this case, as with others, an abundance of verbs reflects the hurried rhythm. The reader and the picaro are rushed from situation to situation at a lightning pace.

3) *Fate Rules Supreme.* The title of chapter six indicates the governing weight of luck in Catrín's life: "En el que se verá cómo empezó a perseguirlo la fortuna y los arbitrios que se dio para burlarse de ella" [In which the reader will see how fortune started to follow him and the measures he took to try to escape it] (p. 47). In spite of his cunning, also mentioned in the title, Catrín never exercises control over his circumstances for any length of time. His penchant for gambling symbolizes his willingness to give himself over wholly to fate. At times luck smiles on him, but fate always exacts its toll eventually, thus making the "Sisyphus rhythm" a very obvious aspect of Catrín's life.

4) *Bodily Violence.* On seven occasions Catrín suffers severe bodily harm. He is kicked, stripped, beaten with a stick, thrown down stairs, whipped, stabbed with a sword, knifed, and has boiling water thrown on him. Catrín precipitates some of these acts of violence, but others he does not. Whatever the case, the punishment always seems greater than the crime.

5a) *A Single Protagonist.* The novel's name fits it well. Don Catrín dominates the entire work.

5b) *Uncommon Origins.* Catrín's origins seem more "normal" than those of classical picaros. He not only has parents as he grows up, but also claims nobility and has documents as proof. However, these claims lose credibility in light of his mother's "dowry," which included two illegitimate children. Although they lacked wealth, his parents provided for Catrín's physical and educational needs.

5c) *Cunning*. Catrín is a clever, resilient individual who thinks on his feet whenever he stands to gain something. Some of the book's most memorable episodes feature his cunning. For example, in one episode Catrín tricks "Simplicio" into buying him several meals and giving him money. To turn the trick, Catrín invents a story about his wealthy, and available, sister. Before being discovered, Catrín actually recruits a "sister" to play the part. Catrín delights in hoodwinking the world, and watching him do so makes enjoyable reading.

5d) *Protean Form*. As Jefferson Rea Spell has stated, Catrín "never entered the service of any master or engaged in any honest occupation."[12] Nonetheless, his list of occupations shows his versatility: student, soldier, gambler, gamester's assistant, thief, salesman (of stolen goods), go-between, and beggar. Indeed, he adapts quickly and proficiently to new roles.

5e) *Alienation*. Through his own vanity and presumption, Catrín distances himself from most of society. He treats others with overt scorn, as inferiors. He sees them as potential host victims for his parasitic ways. His callous happiness when informed of his parents' deaths indicates his isolation from feelings of affection. Only in his relationship with Marcela during the book's final chapters does he encounter anything resembling love. However, when he becomes terminally ill, she abandons him. Catrín is completely alienated from society.

5f) *Internal Instability*. After entering into an altercation and striking a Catholic priest, Catrín states the following: "Algunos aconsejaban que le pidiera perdón . . . pero yo me desentendí, bien satisfecho de que un caballero catrín no debe prostituirse a pedir perdón a nadie" [Some counseled me to ask his forgiveness . . . but I washed my hands of it, fully satisfied that a gentleman dandy should not prostitute himself by asking anyone's forgiveness] (p. 67). As happens throughout the novel, our picaro here displays noteworthy resolve and consistency in acting as a "dandy" should. The remarkable irony which extends throughout the novel turns his apparent stability into mush. A front merely masks Catrín's lack of resolve.

5g) *A Philosophical Bent*. Catrín's education included formal training in philosophy. However, during classes he dedicated himself more to poking fun at the teachers and the discipline than mastering the subject. Occasional semiphilosophical statements dot the text. Although his assertions often lack validity, he definitely has a philosophical bent.

6) *The First-Person Point of View.* Catrín indeed narrates the novel in the "yo" form. This point draws further analysis below.

7) *An Unkind, Chaotic World.* We have noted the violence our picaro encounters during his adventures, but other characters suffer bodily harm as well. Picaros and parasites infest his world and serve as his teachers. For example: "Dos años viví contento, aprendiendo mil primores de mis amigos Tremendo y compañeros. Sus máximas para mí eran el evangelio y sus ejemplos la pauta por donde reglaba mis costumbres" [For two years I lived contentedly, learning a thousand delicacies from my friends Tremendo and his companions. His words were gospel to me and his example was the standard by which I would rule my life] (p. 37). In many respects, Catrín's short-comings merely reflect the society he observes.

8) *Physical Survival.* More than once we find Catrín stripped of all necessities, reduced to pure misery. He speaks often of his lack of food, and several episodes revolve around his attempts to secure a free meal. The picaro's obsession with appearances and clothing provide a twist on this theme, an echo of the "escudero" episode in *Lazarillo de Tormes.* Given money when naked and starving, he would invest first in presumptuous clothes, then worry about sustenance.

9) *A Vast Gallery of Human Types.* Not only are the secondary characters in the novel types, but many of their names reveal their type exactly. For example, "Tremendo" is a big-mouthed soldier who defies authority and constantly chases trouble. "Simplicio" is a simpleton and easy prey for Catrín. "Abundo" is an old man with an abundance of money. Other characters with symbolic names include Precioso, Modesto, and Sagaz [Shrewd]. Many other characters remain nameless, referred to as the priest, the landlord, the mayor, the chaplain, the scribe, etc. Instead of detailed, well-rounded people, the ranks of secondary characters swell with rapidly sketched, lively types.

The times in which *Don Catrín*'s author lived had a major impact on his writings. In fact, the injustices and abuses Lizardi saw in the Mexico of his day drove him to his profession as a writer. The struggle for independence furthered deterioration of economic, social, and political conditions, which undoubtedly intensified his desire for reform.[13] Periodicals and pamphlets provided his initial mode of communication. His attacks targeted the government, incompetent doctors, clergy, civic and social conditions, and the class system. His public zeal for reform made him famous in his day, and led to his well-known pseudonym—El Pensador Mexicano [The Mexican Thinker]. Censors and governmental authorities judged much of what Lizardi wrote openly seditious. In spite of laws proclaiming freedom of the press in Spain and its holdings, officials imprisoned El Pensador on more than one occasion for his writings.[14] In response, Lizardi turned to a new genre, and the novel emerged in Mexico. Although he had turned to a new means of communication, Lizardi never wavered in his passion for reform.

Thus, several factors came into play as Lizardi approached *Don Catrín*. First, societal reform constituted his overarching motive; second, censorship forced him away from pamphlets and journals as his method of communication; and third, even in a novelistic genre his writing had to be approved by the censors. Since the novel did not reach publication until after its composition, we can only speculate as to whether it could have reached print in its day. However, I believe these factors caused Lizardi to adopt certain strategies, some of which key the book's aesthetic and reformational success.

As noted above, a first-person point of view marks the novel. In my opinion, a major key to the novel's success on an artistic level lies in having its protagonist narrate the work. The opening paragraph of the book reveals the first-person narrative technique and part of the narrator's personality:

> Sería yo el hombre más indolente y me haría acreedor a las execraciones del universo, si privara a mis compañeros y amigos de este precioso librito, en cuya composición me he alambicado los sesos, apurando mis no vulgares talentos, mi vasta erudición y mi estilo sublime y sentencioso.

> [I would be the world's most indolent man and would be deserving of the execrations of the universe, if I denied my companions and friends this precious little book, in the composition of which I have distilled my brains, pouring into it my unusual talent, my vast erudition, and my sublime and sententious style] (p. 3).

This paragraph tells us immediately that the narrator's style fits the title of the novel perfectly. The lexicon and syntax go with the given name in their elegance and polish. The content corresponds to the surname. The adjectives he ascribes to himself and his work are presumptuous in quality (*precious* book, *unusual* talent, *sublime* and *sententious* style) and astonishing in quantity (I would be *the world's most* indolent man, the execrations of the *universe,* my *vast* erudition).

The next paragraphs claim *Don Catrín* is a much better book than the *Periquillo* and predict eventual fame: "todo hijo de Adán, sin exceptuar uno solo, al oír el sonoroso y apacible nombre de don Catrín, su único, su eruditísimo autor, rendirá la cerviz y confesará su mérito recomendable" [Each of Adam's descendants, without a single exception, upon hearing the sonorous and placid name of Mr. Dandy, its only, its enormously erudite author, will on bended knee confess his undeniable merit] (pp. 3–4). Here we find that the book's title character and narrator do indeed coincide. His claims increase in boastfulness while maintaining stylistic ostentation. The name's symbolism fits the character absolutely.

The fourth paragraph maintains the same pretentious tone. Catrín states that his purpose in writing his life story is to increase the number of dandies in the world by exhibiting his life as an example. Devoid of all modesty, he justifies this end by bragging of his fairy-tale life: "la de un caballero ilustre por su cuna, sapientísimo por sus letras, opulento por sus riquezas, ejemplar por su conducta, y héroe por todos sus cuatro costados" [that of a gentleman of illustrious heritage, marvelously learned through his studies, opulently wealthy, exemplary in his conduct, and a hero through and through] (p. 4).

In paragraphs five and six he tells of his "noble" lineage and his place and year of birth. Unable to resist an opportunity to boast, he observes that his literary skills and sense of morality are developed well beyond his years, and feels that he is the great hero and prodigy of the eighteenth century. The flagrant presumptuousness of the narrator undoubtedly impresses any reader. Catrín seems absolutely sincere in his outlandish claims. Nevertheless, even though Catrín has not begun to narrate the events of his life, several factors lead us to sense a discrepancy between what is being said and the "reality" of Catrín's life. First, the narrator's name is far from heroic and suggests the negative qualities mirrored in the style of the text. Second, in the third paragraph he mentions his riches and opulence, while in the fifth he admits family poverty. Third, and most important, if his life is tremendously heroic and worthy of our emulation, he spends excessive amounts of time telling us so. We would instead expect any life as admirable as he describes to speak for itself.

Paragraph six signals the beginning of the overt unraveling of our narrator's lofty claims. Because of its importance in the development of irony in the novel, I examine it here in some detail. The paragraph begins with Catrín trifling with words over his parents' poverty, claiming that although they may have been poor, they weren't miserable. This leads to an explanation of his mother's dowry, which includes two illegitimate (albeit engendered from a titled gentleman) children and the money the gentleman gave her to keep quiet about the affair. Sound judgment obviously escapes Catrín—first, in considering illegitimate children part of a dowry and second, in mentioning them while trying to prove his parents' honor. Next, Catrín attempts to justify his father's acceptance of such a dowry, emphasizing that he was aware of the situation and was wise to accept it given the handsome sum of blackmail money—hardly an admirable set of reasons. In the next sentence, Catrín's claim to noble heritage as a result of his mother's dowry shows an absolute lack of correlation between what he says and the facts in his life. Irony has come to the forefront of the novel in just six paragraphs. As if Catrín has not dug enough of a hole for himself in the first four sentences of the paragraph, he crowns it with a fifth:

> Los árboles genealógicos que adornan los brillantes libros de mis ejecutorias, y los puestos que ocuparon mis beneméritos ascendientes en las dos lucidísimas carreras de las armas y las letras, me pondrán *usque in aeternum* a cubierto de las notas de vano y sospechoso, cuando os aseguro a fe de caballero don Catrín que soy noble, ilustre y distinguido, por activa, por pasiva y por impersonal.

> [The genealogical trees that adorn the brilliant books of my career, and the positions which my deserving ancestors held in the two luminous careers of arms and letters, will place me *usque in aeternum* outside the talk of the vain and suspicious, and I assure you on my honor as a gentleman dandy that I am noble, illustrious, and distinguished, actively, passively, and impersonally] (p. 5).

In this sentence, Catrín attempts to claim privileged heritage by virtue of his patent of nobility and his ancestors' honorable professions. Had he left it at this he would have made a point. However, he cannot resist embellishing the sentence as well as the claim; in the process he mires himself in trouble. First, he acknowledges the existence of those who do not consider him noble. Second, he swears on his gentleman's honor that he is a gentleman—a prospect governed by faulty logic. Last, in his final flourish he sets forth in triplicate what he is (noble, illustrious, and distinguished) followed by the ways he is these things, also in triplicate (actively, passively, and impersonally). Such ludicrous, vapid reasons for claiming nobility are heightened by the sentence's syntactic elegance.

By the end of this paragraph the basic narrative situation and personality of the narrator have been established for the rest of the book. Skillful utilization of the first-person narrative strategy creates a sustained distance between what is said and the "reality" of the situation—a standard definition of irony.

In the passages we have just examined, Catrín creates irony on his own by summarizing and commenting on events and situations from his life. This technique frequently surfaces in the novel to create irony. Irony and moralizing also derive from another oft-used technique in the book. Catrín at times quotes secondary characters, thus yielding to their voice in the narrative. For example, he quotes Modesto at some length as to the evils of dueling. The points of his speech ring true and could echo advice for reform from Lizardi himself. Catrín, however, rejects it, and in his self-justification creates further irony. This technique creates the side effect of a pleasant blending and variety of scene and summary.

Three narrative circumstances remove Catrín's first-person point of view from the novel: chapter titles, footnotes, and the conclusion. A third-person point of view marks the titles of each chapter. These usually comprise rapid summaries of the chapter's content, with exceptions in chapters five, nine, and fourteen. Chapter 5's title has too many events to summarize quickly: "Largo pero muy interesante" [Long But Very Interesting]. Chapter 9's title includes a moral judgment: "Escucha y admite unos malditos consejos de un amigo; . . . " [He Listens to and Acts upon some Cursed Advice from a Friend]. Chapter 14's title, though in third-person, utilizes the same sort of irony that pervades the text: " . . . se concluye . . . la narración del fin de la vida de nuestro famoso don Catrín" [. . . thus concludes . . . the narration of the end of the life our our famous Mr. Dandy]. Thus, the voice in the chapter titles, though usually detached, is not always free from judgments and even contributes to the moralizing irony in the book.

Thirteen footnotes form part of the text. Seven merely cite sources, one explains an idiom, one refers the reader to a different part of the book,[15] another introduces a story which is never told (although no such story exists in the text—perhaps the implied editor was commenting on the text's deficiencies), and three consist of overt moralizing. We cannot possibly take the author of these notes to have been Catrín. Although the narrative voice in the body of the text remains constant in tone and perspective, the existence of these notes by an implied author or editor weakens it somewhat. However, we must remember Lizardi's purpose in writing, and admit that even though the notes weaken the overall narrative situation, they strengthen the book's moralizing effect.

The concluding chapter, "Hecha por el practicante" [Written by the Attendant] indeed shifts the voice to the attendant who was caring for Catrín in the hospital at the time of his death. Although he shows compassion for the deceased, he quickly points out Catrín's weaknesses:

> El, a título de bien nacido, quiso aparentar decencia y proporciones que no tenía ni pudo jamás lograr, porque era acérrimo enemigo del trabajo. La holgazanería le redujo a la última miseria, y esto le prostituyó a cometer los crímenes más vergonzosos.

> [He, using a title of nobility, tried to put on airs of nobility that he did not possess nor could he have gained, because he was a bitter enemy of work. Laziness reduced him to the utmost misery, which prostituted him to commit the most shameful crimes] (p. 108).

Lizardi apparently distrusted irony's ability to carry out his purposes alone. The voice here seems to match the one in the footnotes. Using the attendant as his mouthpiece, Lizardi sums up his intent in the book in six words: "¡Pobre Catrín! ¡Ojalá no tenga imitadores!" [Poor Mr. Dandy! I hope he will have no imitators!] (p. 108).

While *Don Catrín de la Fachenda* fulfills its purpose as a vehicle calling for reform, it does not sacrifice aesthetics. Extended irony constitutes the perfect tool of both aesthetics and reform. The author allows his main character's words and claims to be absolutely unsubstantiated by what we know of his life. Rare departures from this first-person strategy detract very little from the strength of the novel. Thus, in a remarkable fusion of successful moralizing, excellent narrative technique, humor through irony, lively, fast-paced episodes and interesting characters, we have a novel that is at once challenging, satisfying, and a delightful reading experience.

6

La vida inútil de Pito Pérez

Wherein José Rubén Romero's little masterpiece, La vida inútil de Pito Pérez, *is placed in its historical context and its picaresque attributes discussed, after which the formation of the work's seemingly simple, yet always entertaining hero, or antihero as the case may be, is studied through the examination of the way character codes intertwine in key passages of the text, revealing a beguiling complexity in the character of Pito Pérez.*

JOSÉ RUBÉN ROMERO'S MASTERPIECE, *LA VIDA INÚTIL DE PITO Pérez* [*The Futile Life of Pito Perez*], was published in 1938.[1] Over a century had elapsed since the publication of a narrative with enough picaresque elements to be classified in the subgenre. Only the *Periquillo* maintains a higher literary profile than *La vida inútil* among Mexican narratives of this type. Within a few years of its publication Romero's text became an immensely popular novel. Although examination of the text in scholarly publications has slowed almost to a halt, Mexicans continue to hold it as a favorite.

In some ways *La vida inútil* exemplifies characteristics prevalent in the world of art, and especially literary art, of the twenties and thirties in Mexico; in other ways, it departs dramatically from art of its time. The administration of Lázaro Cárdenas proved especially conducive to artistic production in all media; mural painting constitutes perhaps the most dramatic manifestation of this production. Orozco, Siquieros, Rivera, and Rufino Tamayo returned to Mexico from abroad; their work blossomed as they were then able to exercise full artistic freedom.[2] These artists' preoccupation with the history of Mexico and their desire to identify Mexicanness parallels the predominant theme of Mexico's literature in the thirties.

Literary art in Mexico in the thirties seemed to react against the avant-garde tendencies of the twenties represented by the

---

The majority of this chapter was published in *Chasqui,* Vol. 20, No. 1 (May 1991), pp. 79–86.

"Contemporáneos" and the "estridentista" groups. These groups sought cosmopolitanism and universality, and examined the individual with an emphasis on his interior; in contrast, regionalism and Mexicanness dominated the thirties, with frequent examination of society as a whole, often with emphasis on its exterior. Several excellent non-novelistic texts from this period illustrate the tendencies of the thirties, including *El perfil del hombre y la cultura en México* [*The Profile of Man and Culture in Mexico*] by Samuel Ramos and *El gesticulador* [*The Imposter*] by Rodolfo Usigli. The Revolution and "indigenismo" constitute two of the predominant themes of the decade's novel, exemplified by *Campamento* [*Camp*], *La luciérnaga* [*The Firefly*], *Tierra* [*Soil*], *El indio* [*The Indian*], and *El resplandor* [*Brightness*], perhaps the best-known novels of the decade.

La vida inútil de Pito Pérez includes many of the foregoing tendencies. For example, the story takes place in the state of Michoacán and an intensely regional flavor permeates the text. The book sharply criticizes church and governmental institutions, giving it an element of social protest. Along the same line, the book opens a window to the problems of the lower classes, a portion of Mexican life that had rarely been glimpsed in its literature. On the other hand, it departs from tendencies of the thirties in several major ways. First, rather than give a panoramic view of society, the text focuses on a single individual, Pito Pérez. Second, the humor in *La vida inútil* contrasts dramatically with the sober and severe literature that dominated the thirties in Mexico. Third, it revives the use of picaresque conventions. Thus, although in some ways Romero's novel represents the tendencies of its era, in others it shows innovation and novelty.

Besides enjoying great popularity within a few years of publication, critics showered *La vida inútil de Pito Pérez* with immediate favorable attention. A rapid survey of critical writing on the novel, which has centered primarily on four lines, highlights some of its strengths. Critics have most often approached the book by looking at its place within the picaresque family. Most of these comments point out Pito Pérez's unique characteristics within the subgenre, while one notes its lack of didacticism compared to other picaresque tales, and another focuses on its unique narrative situation.[3] Another line of criticism deals with the literary style of the book. Several critics have commented on its use of regional language from the state of Michoacán, while others have studied the novel's abundant humor.[4] The third type of criticism examines the novel's protagonist, Pito Pérez. Although some early criticism briefly discusses Pito's bitterness, more recent articles have gone into depth on his psychological makeup and his state of alienation.[5] The fourth major critical approach examines the social issues raised by the book. Critics have noted that these issues not only come to light through the outspoken voice of the picaro, but the choice of a protagonist from the lower classes automatically creates a window to social concerns.[6] Outside these four approaches, one study focuses on the book's symbols and internal structure.[7]

Curiously, the last article dedicated to *La vida inútil* was published in 1977. In spite of the novel's continued popularity among the masses, scholars have not continued to give it critical attention. Perhaps the incredible novelistic production of the "boom" and the period since has caused it to be overlooked or forgotten, but surely this amnesia is only temporary.

Let us now turn our attention to the novel's picaresque elements.

1) *Episodic Plot.* Although the plot of *La vida inútil* does indeed feature episodes, their organization differs from the traditional picaresque novel. Whereas in most picaresque novels the episodes occur in a purely chronological order corresponding to the life events of the picaro, in the novel at hand they do not. The difference stems in part from the presence of a controlling narrator in the text. At the beginning of every chapter the narrator gives a theme to Pito upon which to base that chapter's episodes. Thus, the narrator has a transparent role in manipulating the order of the *récit.* For example, chapter 2 deals with Pito's family life; chapter 6 treats Pito's amorous relationships; chapter 7 has Pito's experiences with jails as its theme, and so forth. In many cases the *récit* appears to follow the chronological order of Pito's *histoire,* but in other cases such a relationship seems unlikely, making an accurate reconstruction of the *histoire* virtually impossible. Even though Pito narrates the events of his life in a thematic fashion rather than in the traditional chronological one, the plot remains episodic. Pito's anecdotes remain almost totally insulated one from another, thus preventing any cause-and-effect relationships common to a realist novel. The presence of Pito himself constitutes the only consistent link between episodes. Thus, *La vida inútil* is fully episodic even though the episodes are arranged thematically rather than chronologically.

2) *Dizzying Rhythm.* Although Pito relates a great number of anecdotes, the rhythm hardly seems vertiginous. This stems

from the thematic organization already noted. Since we remain unaware of the order of the events, neither do we see the pace with which they occurred. The organization lends itself to the picaro approaching his life events from a more philosophical point of view. Thus, we do not feel swept up by the pace of the events as with other picaresque narratives.

3) *Fate Rules Supreme.* Early on Pito points out the power of fate in his life: "My bad luck has followed me since the day I was born and everything I try comes out just the reverse from what I wanted" (p. 8). Although he sometimes attributes his luck to God's will rather than to fate itself, Pito nevertheless frames himself a victim of forces greater than himself. Pito occasionally brings on his own misfortunes, but not always. For example, being the third son in his family dooms him to a life of dead-end employment since his parents spend their ambitions for solid employment on their first two sons. Whereas the family has Pito's older brothers trained to be a priest and a lawyer, respectively, Pito qualifies only as an altar boy. The Sisyphus rhythm, present in many of the text's episodes, also adds weight to fate's hand.

4) *Bodily Violence.* Only once does Pito fall victim to bodily violence, and he brings it upon himself. This episode is discussed below. Compared to the traditional picaro, Pito suffers little physical violence.

5a) *A Single Protagonist.* Pito is indeed the work's only possible protagonist. All other characters appear briefly only once or twice. The book's title accurately claims to portray Pito's life.

5b) *Uncommon Origins.* Pito's origins are less than desirable, to say the least. He never mentions his father, and his mother never nurtured him. Townspeople consider all five of his sisters mad, demented, or deranged, and probably with good reason. Thus, Pito's home-life roots could hardly be called common.

5c) *Cunning.* Pito's cunning becomes immediately apparent in his ability to express himself. His stories, often laced with double meanings, and sometimes pointed aggressively at his listener, always entertain. Besides poking fun at others, he uses his craftiness to keep from starvation, such as when he swindles the owner of a store out of a large square of sugar when the owner thought he would dispense a mere sugar cube. He then states: "This was my first conquest of stupid people" (p. 26). However, Pito uses his talent and ingeniousness most often to obtain alcohol. For example, he manages to siphon almost an entire barrel of wine from a bar by fashioning a hole in the barrel, drinking through a tube concealed in his jacket, then sealing the hole with wax until the next opportunity. Pito does indeed demonstrate remarkable cunning throughout the text.

5d) *Protean Form.* Pito adeptly plays numerous roles in order to survive. His roles include altar boy, assistant to a druggist, professional story teller, assistant to a priest, secretary, store clerk, preacher, journalist, and actor. Never does our protagonist function in any one role for extended periods of time. Nonetheless, he displays impressive versatility in his journey through life.

5e) *Alienation.* From his earliest days, Pito lacks any caring relationships even with his family. This lack of love and concern in his life seems to intensify as he grows older. This subject is further discussed below.

5f) *Internal Instability.* Pito's inability to hold down any job confirms his interior instability. Alcohol constitutes the only anchor in his life.

5g) *A Philosophical Bent.* As evidenced below, Pito is a very observant, keen individual who sees society and its constituents with clarity. He does indeed have a philosophical bent.

6) *The First-person Point of View.* As was noted by Wicks, the narrative situation in *La vida inútil* does not follow exactly that of the classical picaresque novel. Rather, its slight variation features some attractive possibilities. Two voices, both in first-person, are present in the work—that of the controlling narrator, and that of the protagonist. The narrator serves mainly as a framing device. His conversations with Pito make up almost the entire text. Most sections begin with his presence, but he disappears upon yielding to Pito during most of the text.

7) *An Unkind, Chaotic World. La vida inútil* takes place in the state of Michoacán, Mexico, within several decades of the conclusion of the revolution. At one point Pito points to the jails of the region as his favorite places. Such a statement testifies to the unkind nature of the world he inhabits.

8) *Physical Survival.* When Pito was born, a baby was also born to a friend of Pito's mother. This friend subsequently died. Out of charity, Pito's mother became the baby's guardian and wet nurse. Since his mother would feed the other baby first, from the time he was born Pito knew hunger. Although not a dominant theme in the text, hunger does occasionally surface.

Often, Pito responds to hunger by drinking himself into oblivion.

9)   *A Vast Gallery of Human Types.* The supporting cast in Pito's adventures consists of a variety of types depicted in brief but colorful terms. Some of the outstanding secondary figures who make up this gallery are Padre Coscorrón [Father Rapper], appropriately named because of the stinging blows he administers to the heads of the altar boys; José de Jesús Jiménez, the incredibly obese druggist who goes to any length to avoid rising from his chair; Jiménez's wife, Jovita Jaramillo, who deceives her husband with Pito while the cuckold sits perched on his chair in the next room; Vásquez, a public administrator who by day steals Pito's ideas without acknowledging them and who becomes a champion guzzler by night; and Don Santiago, a rich young man who steals Pito's girlfriend to marry her. The gallery of human types is one of *La vida inútil*'s entertaining, and revealing, aspects.

Several of the critics referred to above mentioned *La vida inútil*'s appeal. Undoubtedly an abundance of humor in the book is one of its major attractions. Nonetheless, this constitutes only a portion of the novel's allure. Ewart E. Phillips strikes at the heart of the matter when he claims that Pito Pérez is the most popular fictional character in Mexican literature.[8] Although this statement appeared in 1964, it continues to ring true today. Along the same line, Manuel Pedro González observes that Romero's novels are among the few Mexican novels written before 1940 which have universal appeal. He states that foreigners easily identify with their humble characters, and that the author "ha sabido descubrir lo que en el campesino michoacano hay de esencia humano, de universal y permanente" [has managed to bring to light in a peasant from Michoacán those things that are fundamentally human, universal, and permanent].[9] These observations on Romero's characters in general apply perfectly to the individual case of Pito Pérez. The presentation of the book's protagonist not only explains its appeal, but reveals Romero's skill as an author.

In the remainder of this study I give evidence which substantiates the observations made by González; in turn, this evidence provides rationale for Pito Pérez's enduring popularity. Thus, it sheds light on the book's lasting magnetism and allows a glimpse into its mastery. I use here a variation on an approach created by Roland Barthes and exemplified in his book, *S/Z*.[10] In the introduction to *S/Z*, Barthes states that in worthwhile texts, the networks are many and interact, without any one of them being able to surpass the rest; . . . we gain access to it by several entrances, none of which can be authoritatively declared to be the main one; the codes it mobilizes extend as far as the eye can reach . . .[11]

Although an infinite number of codes intertwine in each of the many "networks" of any text, any manageable interpretation thereof can examine only a limited number of codes. In *S/Z,* for example, Barthes works with only five codes. Inasmuch as González and Phillips suggest that strong characterization of the protagonist is the richest asset of *La vida inútil de Pito Pérez,* I will focus on this "network." Within it I highlight five codes whose presence and interaction reveal the depth of Pito Pérez:

1. NARRATOR'S PERCEPTION OF PITO

This code alone is manifest exclusively through the interventions of the narrator. The narrator's overt role in the text is limited, for he generously yields more than ninety percent of the text directly to the protagonist himself. In fact, in some chapters the narrator disappears. Nevertheless, his few words add a great deal to our appreciation of Pito, to a large degree because they provide us with a point of view outside the character.

2. PITO'S SOCIAL CONSCIENCE

Much of what Pito says can be classified as philosophy or social criticism. Without this serious side to the character, he would probably be nothing but a caricature. This dimension enriches our concept of the protagonist and gives him a degree of intellectual depth. Although presented in the words of the protagonist, this code seems to correspond to the book's author, whereby he voices his concerns regarding political and social institutions.

3. PITO'S SENSE OF IRONY

The presence of humor in Pito's narrations constitute one of the main reasons for his popularity. Nevertheless, humor never dominates the text, but rather interweaves with very serious codes throughout. In spite of an abundance of humor, the text is never allowed to become overly giddy, but remains focused on social issues.

4. Pito's Alienated Condition

Most of the episodes in the novel conclude with Pito experiencing both physical and emotional separation from his fellow characters. Thus, the text chronicles his ever-increasing alienation in a stark, intertwining counterpoint to the code of irony. This element discretely creates sympathy for Pito without in turn alienating the reader, because rather than making an overt plea for pity, he is presented in lamentable predicaments. This code adds an emotional dimension to the character and to the reader's experience.

5. Pito's Attitude of Defiance

Using the ideas set forth by Genette, the nuclear sentence in the text is "Pito defies the conventions of society."[12] His nonconformity constitutes a fundamental part of his personality. This code relates closely to the code of alienation on two counts, because not only does Pito's alienation lead him to rebel, but these acts of recalcitrance, in turn, further isolate him.

Barthes' theory of "codes and networks" is, by his own admission, unwieldy for several reasons. Not only are the networks numerous and the codes therein infinite, but in theory the entire text "should" (theoretically) be analyzed. For illustrative purposes, Barthes's critique of "Sarrasine" is six times longer than the original text. At the same rate, complete interpretation of even a relatively short novel such as *La vida inútil de Pito Pérez* would generate a tome of more than a thousand pages. To avoid such excess, I selected the following passages (or in Barthes' terminology, "lexias") from the text as they illustrate the interweaving of the above codes while also representing key passages in the presentation of Pito Pérez.

> Lexia 1.   Sus grandes zapatones rotos hacían muecas de dolor; su pantalón parecía confeccionado con telarañas, y su chaqueta, abrochada con un alfiler de seguridad, pedía socorro por todas las abiertas costuras sin que sus gritos lograran la conmiseración de las gentes (p. 11).
>
> [His bulky, ill-fitting shoes had come apart and they seemed to grimace as if in pain. His pants appeared to have been made of cobwebs and his jacket, fas-

tened in front with a safety pin, cried out for help through all its open seams. But its pleas did not stir the pity of the people] (p. 3).

NARRATOR'S PERCEPTION OF PITO/PITO'S ALIENATED CONDITION

This passage, the first physical description of Pito in the novel, shows the narrator's poetic style, even though he describes a mere vagabond. The code of alienation is masterfully introduced on the text's opening page through personification—the ability to cry out is attributed to the protagonist's ragged jacket. The fact that the jacket fails to arouse compassion foreshadows the events of the entire novel.

LEXIA 2.   ¿No ha observado usted que la profesión de déspota es más fácil que la de médico o la de abogado? Primer año: ciclo de promesas, sonrisas y cortesías para los electores; segundo año: liquidación de viejas amistades para evitar que con su presencia recuerden el pasado, y creación de un Supremo Consejo de Lambiscones; tercer año: curso completo de egolatría y megalomanía; cuarto y último año: preponderancia de la opinión personal y arbitrariedades a toda orquesta (p. 14).

[Haven't you ever noticed that the profession of being a tyrant is much easier than being a physician or a lawyer? First year: an endless cycle of promises, smiles, and courteous words to those who elected him; second year: ending old friendships or paying off old friends to avoid being reminded of the past by their presence, and creating a Supreme Council of Brown Nosers; third year: complete courses in self-worship and delusions of grandeur; fourth and final year: complete predominance of personal opinions and abuses of all kinds] (p. 5).

PITO'S SOCIAL CONSCIENCE/PITO'S SENSE OF IRONY/PITO'S ATTITUDE OF REBELLION

The voice in this lexia, in which the code of social conscience dominates, is entirely Pito's. Pito has obviously paid close attention to the political situation in Mexico. At the same time, the protagonist's intelligence is patent in his speech, which shows a degree of intellectual depth. The philosophical pessimism in the passage interacts with the code of irony; as a result, reading the text is not an oppressive experience. On the contrary, we admire Pito's verbal grace. At the same time, we see in this passage the protagonist's attitude of defiance in that he dares to speak out against political authorities.

LEXIA 3.   "—Pito Pérez, ponte de rodillas y reza el *Yo pecador* para confesarte: ¿Quién se robó el dinero de Nuestro Señor?"
"—No sé, padre".
"—*Hic et nunc* te condeno si no me dices quién es el ladrón . . ."
"—Yo fui, Padre"—exclamé con un tono angustiado, temoroso de aquellas palabras en latín que no entendía, y que por lo mismo pareciéronme formidables (p. 32).

["Pito Perez! Get down on your knees! Pray for forgiveness and then confess: Who stole Our Saviour's money?"
"I don't know, Father."
"*Hic et nunc* I shall condemn you to Hell if you don't tell me who the thief is."
"It was I, Father!" I exclaimed in anguish, frightened beyond description by those Latin words I didn't understand and that therefore seemed very formidible to me] (p. 19).

PITO'S ALIENATED CONDITION/PITO'S SENSE OF IRONY/ PITO'S ATTITUDE OF DEFIANCE

The code of alienation pervades this lexia. Pito's isolation as he faces the priest parallels his state with regard to society in general. Padre Coscorrón's use of Latin reminiscent of Doctor Purgante in *El Periquillo Sarniento* provides the passage with a touch of humor. Although the Latin expression ("Here and now") is short and simple, it intimidates Pito into confessing and leads to his further alienation. The code of rebellion interacts indirectly in the passage. In spite of the fact that here he conforms to the will of the clergy, the protagonist finds himself in this predicament because he helped steal donations. In addition, if he were to conform completely to the desires of the priest, he would confess that his friend not only participated in the crime but masterminded it.

LEXIA 4.   ¡Pobres de los pobres! Yo les aconsejo que respeten siempre la ley, y que la cumplan, pero que se orinen en sus representantes (p. 86).

[Oh, pity the poor people! I advise them to respect the law, always, and to obey the law. But, I also advise them to piss on its representatives] (p. 59).

PITO'S SOCIAL CONSCIENCE/PITO'S SENSE OF IRONY/PITO'S ATTITUDE OF DEFIANCE

Pito demonstrates here that he is thinking. He has just recounted the story of a politician who does not concern himself with the poor. His advice to always respect the law surprises us somewhat, since Pito has freely criticized its representatives. Nevertheless, this advice becomes transparently ironic, for it merely prepares us for the grotesque jolt of humor with which the sentence ends. Pito's attitude of defiance underlies his irreverent suggestion.

LEXIA 5.   La humanidad es una hipócrita que pasa la vida alabando a Dios, pretendiendo engañarlo con el Jesús en los labios y maldiciendo y renegando sin piedad del Diablo.
    ¡Pobrecito del Diablo, qué lástima le tengo, porque no ha oído jamás una palabra de compasión o de cariño! (pp. 89–90.)

[Humanity is a hypocrite that spends its life praising God, trying to deceive Him with the word Jesus on its lips and, at the same time, without any pity whatsoever, cursing and denying the Devil.
    Oh, the poor Devil. How sorry I am for him! he has never heard a single word of compassion or of love] (p. 62).

PITO'S ALIENATED CONDITION/PITO'S SOCIAL CONSCIENCE/PITO'S ATTITUDE OF DEFIANCE

Pito observes here society's shallowness and falsity regarding religion. This develops into an extended comparison of the Devil and Jesus Christ. In this discussion Pito expresses great sympathy for the former. His concern for the lack of love shown for the Evil One defines his own alienated situation. The code of Pito's alienated state dominates this section of the book. Of course, the notion of sympathizing with the Devil bares Pito's willingness to defy the norms of a Catholic society.

> LEXIA 6. Al terminar el Secretario, me puse de pie improvisando estos malos versos:
>> El pueblo lo felicita
>> por la mujer que se lleva.
>> Es dadivosa, bonita,
>> diligente, y casi nueva . . .
>
> El novio se puso de pie . . . y cogiendo una botella de sobre la mesa, me la tiró con tal tino que, dándome con ella en la frente, me hizo rodar por el suelo bañado en mi propia sangre (pp. 111–12).

> [When the secretary finished, I stood up and improvised these rather poor verses:
>> And for the wife that you now boast,
>> The town folks drink a friendly toast.
>> She's kind and pretty, and generous too.
>> Oh yes, I forgot—she's almost new . . .
>
> The husband leaped to his feet . . . grabbed a bottle from one of the tables and threw it at me with such dead aim that it hit me squarely in the face and sent me reeling across the floor, bathed in my very own blood] (p. 78).

PITO'S SENSE OF IRONY/PITO'S ALIENATED CONDITION/ PITO'S ATTITUDE OF DEFIANCE

Picaresque defiance coupled with alienation lie at the heart of this passage, which gives the details of a wedding party. Pito goes out of his way to attend the event to take advantage of the free food and the opportunity to publicly shame the bride and groom. She had been Pito's lover, and the groom had betrayed his friendship by stealing his sweetheart. Hence, Pito is doubly alienated, having lost the love of Chucha and the friendship of Santiago. Rather than simply accept his misfortune, Pito strikes out in rebellion against his former confidants through his humorous verses. The groom's violent reaction furthers the protagonist's alienation.

He is left wounded and completely abandoned on the floor. This image is the physical equivalent of Pito's emotional isolation.

LEXIA 7. Sí, es verdad, conozco algunas [cárceles] y no me avergüenza confesarlo. He ido a parar a ellas por borracho y travieso, pero a nadie he matado ni he cometido crímenes de esos que honran a los ricos y hunden a los pobres en largos años de condena. Porque un rico mata y se esconde mientras su dinero quebranta leyes y suaviza voluntades (pp. 115–16).

[Yep, it's true. I know quite a few (jails) from personal experience, and I'm not ashamed to confess this publicly. I have spent a lot of time in them, locked up for being drunk or as a public nuisance. But I have never killed anyone, nor have I committed any of those crimes for which the rich are commended and the poor are sentenced to many years in prison. A rich man kills and then he takes refuge in his hideaway while his money greases palms and buys off the law] (p. 80).

PITO'S SOCIAL CONSCIENCE/PITO'S ALIENATED CONDITION/PITO'S ATTITUDE OF DEFIANCE

These words function as a prologue to a complete chapter dealing with Pito's experiences in jails. Ironically, although alienation dominates, Pito comments in the chapter that behind bars he found an environment of family warmth that he never experienced in his own home. By his own admission, his defiant nature lands him in jail often, but he observes that because he is poor he receives longer terms of punishment than wealthy counterparts. The code of Pito's social conscience is mobilized here as he comments on the injustices of the penal system. Although we do not see it in this segment, humor is interwoven throughout this chapter in spite of its seemingly cheerless subject matter.

LEXIA 8. Debo advertirle, con la honradez que ha caracterizado mi desvergüenza, que ya no soy un borracho respetable, ni siquiera ingenioso. Me escarnecen los chicos, me roban los tenderos, me humillan los gendarmes, y cuando quedo tendido en las banquetas,

> . . . no hay alma caritativa que extienda sobre mis
> desnudeces el abrigo de un periódico (pp. 151–52).

[With the same honesty that has always characterized my shamelessness, I must warn you that I am
no longer a respectable drunk. Not even an ingenious one. Children make fun of me; shopkeepers
rob me; the police humiliate me. And when I'm
stretched out somewhere on some bench, . . . no
kind soul even attempts to cover my nakedness with
a newspaper] (p. 108).

Pito's Sense of Irony/Pito's Alienated Condition

This lexia is taken from the first chapter of the second half of
the book. Ten years have elapsed, and Pito's alienated state is even
more advanced. Even children, usually symbols of unconditional
acceptance, have hardened themselves to him. People now seem
to go out of their way to overtly express their disapproval of him.
Although his sense of irony is more sedate, it shows through in the
first sentence of this lexia. As is represented here, the code of
alienation takes root in this chapter as the predominant one in the
entire second part of the novel.

Lexia 9.   Su estampa era la misma que yo conocí diez años
antes: levita deteriorada con flor en el ojal, bastón
de puño niquelado, pantalón con unas rodilleras tan
amplias que podría guardar en ellas a sus hijos, a
semejanza de los canguros; sombrero carrete haciendo equilibrios para conservarse sobre la melena
alborotada y que por su color de oro viejo, parecía
aureola de santo (pp. 155–56).

[His appearance was the same as I had known it ten
years before: a ragged and worn Prince Albert coat
with a flower in his buttonhole, a cane with a nickle-
plated handle, a pair of trousers so baggy at the
knees that he could have kept his children in them,
just like a kangaroo. He wore his wide-brimmed
straw hat that was balanced precariously on his un-
combed mop of hair and that, because of its color
like old gold, looked just like the halo of a saint]
(p. 110).

NARRATOR'S PERCEPTION OF PITO/PITO'S ALIENATED CONDITION

The voice in this lexia belongs to the narrator rather than Pito. The image of Pito as a saint is particularly striking. This is the second time in the book that he is portrayed with a halo. Either his suffering in alienation has sanctified him or his alienation is so pronounced that he is no longer to be identified with his fellow human beings. The animal imagery used here to describe Pito also suggests that he is so alienated that he should not even be associated with the human race. His physical state now reveals an exterior that reflects an extreme interior alienation.

> LEXIA 10. He sido huésped de un buen número de hospitales en donde, si no mueren los pacientes de la enfermedad que allí los llevó, sucumben de hambre o en algún experimento clínico (p. 158).
>
> [I have been the guest of a goodly number of hospitals where, if the patients don't die of the illness that brought them there in the first place, they succumb to hunger or die the victim of some clinical experiment] (p. 112).

PITO'S SOCIAL CONSCIENCE/PITO'S SENSE OF IRONY/PITO'S ALIENATED CONDITION/PITO'S ATTITUDE OF DEFIANCE

Pito is admitted to hospitals for delirium tremens. Beginning with the first chapter of the novel, alcohol plays an important role in Pito's life. In fact, the entire narrative premise of the text involves liquor. The narrator uses alcohol as currency to pay Pito each time he interviews him. Each conversation constitutes a chapter of the novel. As the narrative progresses, alcohol's importance escalates; in fact, Pito becomes increasingly alienated in direct proportion to his alcoholic dependence. His comments with regard to hospital care are a direct social criticism, and at the same time they reveal a humor rooted in bleak irony. His drunkenness stems from his attitude of defiance, as does his stubborn refusal to die.

> LEXIA 11. Alguno de la tertulia, sonriendo maliciosamente, interrogó a Pito Pérez:
>   "—¿Y la Caneca?
>   "Está en casa, rodeada de comodidades".

—¿Quién es la Caneca?—pregunté intrigado por saber a quién se referían.

—¡El amor más fiel que he tenido en mi vida! (p. 175).

[Smiling maliciously, someone in the group asked Pito Perez:

"And Caneca?"

"She's at home, surrounded by all the comforts of life."

"Who is Caneca?" I asked, curious to find out about this person.

"The most faithful love I have had in all my life!"] (p. 124).

PITO'S SENSE OF IRONY/PITO'S ALIENATED CONDITION

The attitude of the first questioner here shows the contempt others have for Pito. His state of alienation is hardly surprising in light of such an attitude. However, the presence of a faithful lover in Pito's life suggests that he is no longer completely isolated from the love and concern of his fellow man. Nonetheless, as the anecdote continues, we find that this sweetheart is the most powerful symbol of alienation in Pito's life. Caneca is a skeleton that Pito kidnapped in an act of defiance and desperation. On the surface, this situation is surprising and grotesquely ironic, but at a deeper level it is tragic.

LEXIA 12.   Los vecinos madrugadores descubrieron el cadáver sobre un montón de basura, con la melena en desorden, llena de lodo, la boca contraída por un rictus de amargura, y los ojos muy abiertos mirando con altivez desafiadora al firmamento (p. 181).

[The early risers in the neighborhood found the body on a pile of rubbish. Its hair was completely disheveled and caked with mud. Its mouth had contracted into a convulsive grin of bitterness. Its wide-open eyes looked at the heavens with a challenging haughtiness.] (p. 128).

Narrator's Perception of Pito/Pito's Alienated Condition/Pito's Attitude of Defiance

This physical description of Pito's cadaver is movingly pathetic. As a dead man, he is presented in the most alienated state possible—as human refuse. The expression of bitterness on Pito's lips symbolizes his alienation. Appropriately, even in death his eyes reflect the defiance that characterized his life. This final symbol of insolence seems to be against heaven itself, thus leaving behind his rebellion against mere humans.

Brushwood comments: "*La vida inútil de Pito Pérez* is a very entertaining book. It may be a very serious book. . . . [I]n addition to the obvious humor, there is a much more subtle current that rides the line between tragedy and comedy in a wonderful fashion."[13] The foregoing analysis shows that the novel is indeed entertaining yet terribly serious. Although in a study of this length we cannot examine the entire text, the interrelationships of the codes and their relative frequency in the novel are well represented by the sampling given here. The following diagram charts these findings:

LEXIA   CODE

| | Narrator's Perception of Pito | Pito's | | | |
		Social Conscience	Sense of Irony	Alienated Condition	Attitude of Defiance
1	X			X	
2		X	X		X
3			X	X	X
4		X	X		X
5		X		X	X
6			X	X	X
7		X		X	X
8			X	X	
9	X			X	
10		X	X	X	X
11			X	X	
12	X			X	X
Total	3	5	7	10	8

Whereas prior critical writing on *La vida inútil* has compartmentalized the above concepts, we see here their relative weight in the novel. Particularly striking is the predominance of the code of Pito's Alienated Condition, which permeates the text. The symbiotic relationship between Pito's alienation and his rebellious nature is also patent in this diagram. Returning to the question of the novel's appeal, examination of the code of Pito's Sense of Irony is instructive. As is charted above, this code never occurs in an isolated way; rather, it appears in conjunction with one or more of the other codes examined here, each of which represents a profound lack of comicality. Humor does not dominate the text, nor is it a mere counterpoint to seriousness therein; instead, it is integrated masterfully into its seriousness. Its presence in more than half of the lexias examined here is evidence that humor is a major force in the novel; it is indisputably one of its major draws. However, the fact that the text is not just a frolicking escape from reality makes it even more appealing.

The codes examined herein back Manuel Pedro González's assertion that Romero's characters draw on universal traits. Social problems, humor, alienation, and defiance transcend region and nationality. Skillful intertwining of these codes has resulted in a wonderfully complex character with universal magnetism. This study has focused on only a few of the codes and passages and just one "network" of the text. A more extended study would reveal further complexities. In the wake of the "Boom," we must not lose sight of the excellence of many of the texts that preceded it.

7

El Canillitas

Wherein Valle-Arizpe's El Canillitas *is identified as a "colonialista" novel (although the colonialist mode was sixteen years outdated at the time of its publication) and its picaresque characteristics identified, after which analysis is made of the many ways in which the reader is treated to humor in the novel, among which are the narration of practical jokes, the presence of linguistic and situational irony, the use of humorous names and nicknames, the utilization of comical comparisons, and so forth.*

EL CANILLITAS, NOVELA DE BURLAS Y DONAIRES [CANILLITAS, A *Novel of Pranks and Other Attractions*], published in 1941 by Artemio de Valle-Arizpe, features anachronism on several counts.[1] The novel takes place in colonial Mexico, it uses archaic language, and an antiquated flavor permeates the text. One would think that Valle-Arizpe wrote it between 1918 and 1926, when novelists cultivated the *colonialista* novel in Mexico. While other authors of colonialist novels created other types of fiction after 1926, Valle-Arizpe continued in the same mode throughout his lifetime. *El Canillitas* represents just one fruit of his incessant effort.

Almost all of the Mexican fiction written in the 1930s and early 1940s deals with twentieth-century Mexico. Whereas *La vida inútil de Pito Pérez* takes a mere backward glance in terms of the picaresque conventions it employs, *El Canillitas,* written just three years later, immerses itself in the past. Although the work is an oddity when viewed in the context of the development of Mexican fiction, a brief look at its author's career shows that it conforms neatly to Valle-Arizpe's monumental production. Whether he was writing fiction, narrating history or collecting chronicles, legends, and narratives, almost the entirety of his sixty-plus volume work deals with Mexico's Colonial Era. In fact, his special interest in the country's capital city earned him the title of "Cronista de la Ciudad de México" [Chronicler of Mexico City] in 1942. *El Canillitas,* with its precious language, colonial setting, and picaresque model, departs radically from the fiction of the day but reflects accurately its author's preferences.

Within five years of its initial publication, the fourth printing of *El Canillitas* occurred. A more recent edition appeared in 1990. Despite its popularity with the reading public, critics have almost completely overlooked the book. Several factors seem responsible for its lack of critical attention. First, Valle-Arizpe's prominence as a historian casts his fictional works into obscurity. While quality and quantity distinguish his historical work on Colonial Mexico, none of his fictional texts truly shine. Second, the vastness of Valle-Arizpe's work can make any one of his books look like just one more volume by a prolific writer. Third, the fact that colonialist literature had been outmoded in public taste for almost two decades can make a critic see the book as a mere curiosity. Finally, John Brushwood's statement on the colonialist novel applies perfectly to *El Canillitas*: "Judging the colonialist novels from the standpoint of reading pleasure, the only just statement is to say that a little is delightful, but a little goes a long way."[2] All of these factors contribute to *El Canillitas*'s lack of critical attention.

Very few critics have commented on *El Canillitas*. Ermilo Abreu Gómez, in his review of the book, notes its picaresque characteristics and its archaic, academic nature. He considers the book an escape from everyday life into the past, and a cynical, caricaturesque expression of the human condition.[3] Manuel Pedro González thinks that Valle-Arizpe treats the world of the picaresque as an erudite exercise, utilized more for its historical possibilities than as something coming from his heart.[4] Roberto Maximiano Acevedo observed that the author filled his fiction in general with "minute details of the customs, manners, mores, and conventions of those times, giving the most interesting descriptions of the costumes, furnishings, decorations, foods, medications and all aspects of everyday life."[5] This generalized statement on the whole of Valle-Arizpe's fiction applies absolutely to *El Canillitas*.

Let us now turn to an examination of the work's picaresque characteristics.

1) *Episodic Plot.* As with other picaresque novels, *El Canillitas*'s structure depends on its picaro as the only consistent link between chapters. Whereas most of the novel is absolutely episodic, Valle-Arizpe's obsession for presenting details from Mexico's Colonial Era occasionally turns an episode into an exposition on eighteenth-century Mexico City's culture. For example, in the seventh "tranco" (the book has twenty-four "trancos," or strides), the picaro does nothing more than walk from the cathedral across the main square. This chapter, the

longest in the book, describes the cathedral, the plaza, and the people Félix sees on his short walk, including fellow picaros, Indians, peddlers, criminals, beggars, noblemen, and so forth. In spite of an emphasis on manners and customs in this and other similar sections, *El Canillitas*'s plot remains episodic.

2) *Dizzying Rhythm.* Valle-Arizpe's *costumbrista* bent makes the pace of the narrative less than dazzling. In spite of the snail's rate of narration regarding the events of the picaro's life, dizziness can on occasion overcome the reader as a result of the book's excessive length or the overwrought attention to Colonial detail.

3) *Fate Rules Supreme.* Very few references to fate occur in the text of *El Canillitas.* On one occasion the narrator mentions the protagonist's "estrellas contrarias" [unlucky stars] (p. 278). In an unrelated episode, Félix happens to overhear part of a conversation between two judges, during which one says to the other: "De los cinco criminales que hoy hemos condenado a muerte inapelable, tengo la plena seguridad de que dos de ellos sí la merecían" [Of the five criminals we have sentenced to die without appeal, I am completely confident that two of them so deserved] (p. 72). Notwithstanding isolated references such as these to fate, its hand is never emphasized and seldom present. Our protagonist places himself in misfortune's way without needing fate's assistance.

4) *Bodily Violence.* At least ten times in the text Félix falls victim to some form of physical beating. On one occasion, as the victim of a practical joke, he delivers a seemingly innocent message. The message infuriates the storekeeper, who turns on the protagonist and batters him. In another episode, a scuffle escalates into a rock-throwing contest, resulting in Félix's broken skull. Jailmates perform initiation rites on him, thoroughly humiliating him through verbal and physical abuse. When his girlfriend's father catches him in her room, he beats Félix mercilessly. Even men of the cloth in a monastery beat him soundly, albeit in a Christian way. In short, Félix repeatedly experiences bodily violence.

5a) *A Single Protagonist.* In spite of its "costumbrista" tendencies, at its heart *El Canillitas* tells a picaro's story.

5b) *Uncommon Origins.* The text's first "tranco" presents Félix's parents. Although his father's identity was impossible to ascertain with authority, "según fieles cálculos de comadres sabidoras, fue un tal Serapio el Mochilón, ladrón corriente y moliente" [according to the faithful calculations of wise gos-

sips, he was a certain Serapio el Mochilón, a common thief]
(p. 9). Physically lacking in beauty and ever inebriated, Serapio was hanged for murder. Félix's mother hailed from the
same social fabric as his presumed father. Her profession as
a prostitute made childhood stability impossible for the protagonist. Her death made Félix an orphan at a very young
age, after which his mother's fellow-workers raised him in
reprehensible conditions. Félix's peculiar origins hardly prepare him for a stable life.

5c) *Cunning*. Although not emphasized in the text, we easily perceive the picaro's cunning. Early in the narrative we witness
Félix's capacity to turn circumstances to his advantage. A
priest who takes him in gives him the responsibility of passing
the alms basin during mass. As an incentive to inspire hard
work, he offers our protagonist half a "real" for each "peso"
collected. Félix works out a unique interpretation of the offer:

> Apenas se reunió un peso, en el acto extrajo Félix el medio real
> prometido, con lo que quedaron siete y medio; se acabaló, poco
> después, un nuevo peso, es decir ocho reales, y volvió a extraer
> Felisillos su comisión y la siguió sacando apenas se llegaba a esa
> cantidad. De este modo nunca se pasaba en el plato petitorio de
> los siete reales y medio.

> [As soon as a peso was collected, Félix took out the promised
> half-real, leaving seven and a half; moments later additions com-
> pleted the peso, and Felisillo again removed his commission, and
> he continued removing it whenever it reached that amount. Using
> this method the plate never had more than seven and a half re-
> als] (p. 33).

Félix's craftiness brings him many free drinks, free food, and
even a free pulled tooth.

5d) *Protean Form*. Early in his life Félix works in several different
professions. As a young boy, while he lives in a brothel, he
performs a variety of odd jobs ranging from cleaning rooms
to procuring customers. Later he becomes an altar boy, then
a pharmacist's assistant, and still later an amanuensis. He
works in each of these professions for very brief spans. Most
of his life he lives from drink to drink as a jobless vagabond.
Thus, in spite of some role-playing early in his life, overall
Félix does not stand out as a character who plays many roles.

5e) *Alienation*. Without a doubt there are moments in Félix's life
in which he is completely alone, without love or friendship.

His fondness for alcohol further distances him from his fellow man. For example, on one occasion a member of the opposite sex pursues him, but he has lost all capacity for feeling through a constant drunken stupor. Ironically, Félix endures alienation without solitude. As a boy, people take him in or he finds company among fellow picaros; later in life he inevitably has a drinking companion. Despite almost constant companionship, his relationships never endure and lack loyalty and nurturing.

5f) *Internal Instability.* Félix's inability to hold a job stems from his lack of internal stability. In the book's penultimate and antepenultimate chapters he completely gives up drinking. Nevertheless, in the final chapter he repents of his sobriety, negating any equilibrium he had reached. The epitaph on his grave marker summarizes his life's lack of internal drive: "Aquí descansa Félix Vargas, quien siempre descansó" [Here rests Félix Vargas, who always rested] (p. 366). Our protagonist has absolutely no goals, no drive, and no direction.

5g) *A Philosophical Bent.* The only form of philosophy we find in *El Canillitas* comes from the narrator rather than from the protagonist. Furthermore, the narrator's philosophy is not heavy-handed, scholarly, and pedantic, but light, homespun, and often flippant. Short philosophical aphorisms dot the text, such as "quien bien duerme, pulgas no siente" [he who sleeps well feels no fleas] (p. 46) and "ya se sabe que hecha la ley, se hace la trampa" [it is well-known that once a law is made, so are loopholes] (p. 53). Such maxims do not constitute detailed philosophical expositions, but they reveal in the narrator a definite philosophical temperament.

6) *The First-person Point of View.* Valle-Arizpe does not employ the first-person point of view in *El Canillitas.* Instead, a third-person narrator tells the picaro's story in the past tense. The narrator's frequent use of diminutives in reference to the protagonist, especially in the first half of the text, belies his affection for the character. Furthermore, the text is often focalized through Félix. Nonetheless, even though the narrator does not employ strict, cold objectivity, the protagonist does not tell his own story.

7) *An Unkind, Chaotic World.* Fellow picaros, beggars, poverty, filth, and cruelty encompass Félix's world. He becomes acquainted with even the city's most ignominious prison, which houses the lowest grade of person the city can offer. Order

and kindness, though not completely absent from Félix's world, do not figure prominently therein.

8) *Physical Survival.* During the novel, the narrator describes Félix's hunger as eternal, always alert, never appeased, and furious. It maintains a high profile presence during the course of the narration. Our hero's strategy to drown it in alcohol constitutes a poor solution at best. El Canillitas's incessant hunger results in incredible emaciation, earning him the nickname of a human thread. Physical survival does indeed play a prominent role in the text.

9) *A Vast Gallery of Human Types.* Calling the gallery of human types presented in *El Canillitas* vast constitutes a gross understatement. Vast describes the gallery of types presented in chapter seven alone. The text portrays beggars, prostitutes, pharmacists, doctors, men of the cloth, drunks, convicted criminals, picaros, teachers, students, gossips, businessmen, Indians, peddlers, and noblemen, among others. In almost every case, each type takes life in specific characters, whether fairly well developed or scarcely mentioned, named or nameless. For example, Don Libario Liébana, an obese, outspoken, eccentric priest who runs people from his church midweek because he considers them lazy, is a fairly rounded character. On the other hand, the convicts we meet while Félix does time in jail remain types. In the space of three pages we meet twenty-five of them by name with a brief description of their crime or specialization. The extensive array of human types in *El Canillitas* constitutes one of the book's richest elements.

The strong doses of humor incorporated in classic picaresque novels constitute one reason why they have remained popular after several centuries. Evidenced by some of the passages already cited in this study, *El Canillitas* follows in the picaresque novel's tradition of humor. In fact, humor's presence throughout the book comprises not only one of its most appealing characteristics, but one of its most accomplished as well. Let us now analyze some of the devices utilized in the text to produce humor.

Perhaps the type of humor most commonly associated with the picaresque tradition stems from the action of the plot itself. *El Canillitas* features plenty of humor stemming from trickery and ingenuity, as in the following examples. Félix hears students tell how they placed a donkey in their teacher's lecturing seat. When the teacher arrived, the students were paying the same amount of attention to the animal (as they usually did) to their teacher. Turning the tables on them, the teacher:

> fingió no ver al esquelético animal . . . con toda calma se puso a pasar lista y al terminar de leerla se quedó examinando con mucha atención a la bestia, . . . dijo con un fingido asombro:
> —Me he quedado sorprendido, señores míos, de que no figure en mis listas el nombre de este buen compañero vuestro.

> [he pretended to not see the bony animal . . . calmly called roll and upon finishing riveted his attention on the beast, . . . said with feigned astonishment:
> —I am surprised, gentlemen, that my list seems to be lacking the name of this good colleague of yours.] (p. 124)

As Félix works in a pharmacy a stranger arrives and asks our hero to lend him an emetic. The stranger explains, "únicamente lo pido prestado, pues créame, se lo devolveré pronto" (146) [I only ask to borrow it, because believe me, I will return it to you promptly]. After Félix naively lends him the emetic, the man fulfills his promise, but by using the meaning of the word "devolver" [to vomit], which Félix had not anticipated. When Félix has a terribly intense toothache and an equally intense hunger, he makes a clever bet with a man that both ends his toothache and satisfies his hunger. Félix bets that he can eat everything in the restaurant they are frequenting. If he wins, the man pays for the food; if he loses, the man can pull one of his teeth. Félix's intentional loss after stuffing himself actually constitutes a double victory.

Situational humor such as illustrated above, though clever, is not *El Canillitas*'s strongest suit in quantity or subtlety. The use of both linguistic and situational irony constitutes the other type of humor present in this text as well as in many picaresque texts. Ironic statements by the narrator fill the pages of *El Canillitas*. On numerous occasions irony pervades positive adjectives, such as with the "noble oficio" [noble profession] of beggars, Félix's "esclarecidos progenitores" [illustrious forebears], a "buen regalo" [fine gift] consisting of bedbugs, fleas, and lice, "exquisito dialecto de presidio" [exquisite prison dialect], and so forth.

Sometimes irony develops through more than just one word, as in the description of the presumptuous doctor, Aniceto Valdivieso: "el único dueño de la verdad absoluta. Lo que decía era ya cuerpo jurídico para toda cuestión que ocurriese después" [the only owner of absolute truth. Whatever he pronounced became the entire legal precedent for any matter that later surfaced] (pp. 147–48). The same type of irony leads the narrator to refer ironically to many of Félix's experiences in terms of education. From prostitutes he learns "lindas, excelentes cosas que le sirvieron en su bachillerato de pícaro y luego en su doctorado" [lovely, excellent things which benefited him in his Bachelor's degree as a picaro, and later in his doctorate] (pp. 24–25). His time in jail turned him into a "doctor prematuro en muchas nobles artes" [premature doctor in many noble arts] since he was taught by "eximios maestros en todas la disciplinas, quienes enseñaron al mancebo cosas fundamentales. En esos catedráticos de condición rahez no tenía fin su ciencia ni número su sabiduría" [eminent teachers in all disciplines, who taught the young man all things fundamental. Those professors of questionable reputation possessed endless knowledge and infinite wisdom] (p. 159). After his release from prison he meets a new set of distinguished teachers, under which he becomes a "consumado doctor en bellaquería" [full-fledged doctor of roguishness] (p. 175).

Situational irony does not abound in the text, but it occasionally spices the text. Such irony frequently involves religion, as when Félix receives a brutal beating at the hands of friars. Another irony arises in the activities of the undesirables who congregate at the rear of the cathedral. Before taking any actions they piously pray to any of a variety of saints depending on what ignoble undertaking they have planned. For example, they pray to the Virgin of Soledad for success in their burglaries; they implore Saint Judas to keep law-enforcement representatives far from them. Thus, both linguistic and situational irony play strong roles in the text.

El Canillitas features a great many humorous names and nicknames. Some of the characters have names that in and of themselves either suggest the characters' characteristics, fit them ironically, or just sound funny. The name of Mexico City's most effective slanderer, Pablo Longorio de la Rada Rayada [Pablo Longorio of the Underlined Inlet], suggests his lengthy discourses and his mouth the size of a bay. Félix's mother's name, María la Brincos [María the Jumper], represents her willingness to leap freely from man to man. Sidronio Salmerón de Caravantes's given name accurately suggests his penchant for drinking [sidra is a kind of hard apple cider], while his first surname ironically suggests religiosity [similar to Solomon]. The names of Geripundio, Liborio Liébana, Filogonio Azcárate, and Serapio simply sound comic.

The title of the book—the protagonist's nickname—reflects the predominant way in which the narrator refers to characters in the text. We know relatively few characters in the text exclusively by their true names. In contrast, we know no more than the nickname of numerous characters, while others have both a legal name and a nickname. Félix receives his nickname from a woman friend, and it obviously relates to his caricaturesque lack of size: "Un suspiro tenía más carne que Félix el Canillitas, que ostentaba toda su estructura ósea por encima del pellejo" [A breath possessed more flesh than Félix the Shinbone, whose entire bone structure was evident from outside his skin] (p. 191).

As with our hero, other nicknames stem from characters' physical appearance, such as in the case of a gentleman nicknamed "Amapola" [poppy] due to his always red face, the sisters so physically different from each other that they are ironically known as the "Fiel Contraste" [Faithful Contrast], and a man named "El Terror" because of the terrifyingly large size of his nose. A character with a mouth slightly off to one side has an ingenious nickname reflecting this physical peculiarity: "el peón de Ajedrez . . . porque andaba de frente y comía de lado" [the chess pawn . . . because he walked forward and ate sideways] (p. 230).

While some nicknames openly attack certain characters' personalities and reputations, as with "don Pendejo el magnífico" [Sir Idiot the Magnificent], irony tempers others, such as with "el Mudo" [the mute one], so called because in spite of his incessant talking, he never says anything. Many of the text's most amusing nicknames mean very little without explanations revealing their logic and genius. Examples of this type include a prostitute known as "la Tos" [the cough] because "todos la habían tenido" [everyone had had her] (p. 181), and "El Apenitas" [Mr. Barely], so named because "era muy tímido, muy humilde y callado" [he was very timid, humble, and quiet] (p. 160). Other nicknames lack an explanation, and thus come across as colorful, flamboyant, and entertaining, such as with "El Gallo Verde" [The Green Rooster], "Madam Trompadur," "don Quirileisón," and the prisoner known as "Medialuz" [Halflight]. Whether based on physical or behavioral characteristics, and whether an explanation enriches them or not, the names and nicknames given the characters in *El Canillitas* create consistent delight to readers.

Comparison, especially when used to introduce new characters, comprises another technique used to produce humor in the text. These comparisons provide concrete examples that illustrate adjectives or concepts, thus making them more visible and palpable to the reader. The type of comparison most frequently employed in *El Canillitas* equates an aspect of a person or thing with another, such as in the case of a woman who is hot as a stove. Rather than flatly state that Félix's face was wrinkled, a humorous comparison gives this concept a visual and tactile existence: "la cara se le plegaba como acordeón" [his face had folds like an accordion] (p. 260). Also referring to Félix, the narrator states that "parecía cepillo de dientes, porque no tenía más que hueso y pelo" [he looked like a toothbrush because he was no more than a stick and hair] (p. 176). Saying that a group of picaros was everywhere would be a lifeless commentary and would cause no mental stimulation. Adding a ridiculous comparison breathes life into the idea: "se metía por todas partes como humedad" [they got into everything like humidity] (p. 48). A man fat as a pyramid, a woman juicy as a peach, and a man who drinks with the thirst of a tired camel further exemplify how humorous comparisons of equality in the text both tickle our funny bone because of unexpected linking of heretofore completely unlike items, and effectively fill out our mental and emotional image of the items described.

Comparisons of inequality abound almost as much as those of equality in *El Canillitas*. Both types function on the principles mentioned above, but comparisons of inequality have a slightly greater impact both as humor and in creating effective mental images. The following passage contains two such comparisons, along with three instances of ironic adjectives, and two humorous nicknames:

> El tal Nalga de Palo, que tenía lengua más larga que una bandera, hizo de la pindonga madre del Mochilón, ilustre abuela de Félix, un recuerdo afectuoso, muy delicado, diciéndole que fue más transitada que la calle de los Plateros.

> [So called Mr. Stick Buttock, whose tongue was longer than a flag, made an affectionate, delicate remark about the mother of Mochilón, the illustrious grandmother of Félix, saying that her body was more frequented than Plateros street] (p. 13).

The visual image of Félix staggering after too many drinks is greatly enriched by this comparison: "se bamboleaba más que caña en vendaval" [he swayed more than sugarcane in a windstorm] (p. 260). Some comparisons exaggerate, creating a humorous and suggestive impact in readers, such as in this description of the aggressive encounter between two of the text's women: "Fue tal el jollín que armaron, que al lado de él no sería nada lo que hicieran los cuatro jinetes del Apocalipsis" [They made such a disturbance that the destruction of the four horsemen of the Apocalype would pale in comparison] (p. 20). Humorous comparisons of equality and inequality constitute highly effective narrative tools.

El Canillitas employs lists with great regularity in the text as an effective stylistic device. For example, we mentioned above the extensive list of types of prisoners Félix encountered during his stay in jail. Other lists include 124 ways of referring to prostitutes, more than fifty food dishes prepared by the priest's servant, more than twenty terms used to indicate racial mixtures, things the pharmacist does, things heard on the street, religious events, and so forth. Many of these lists have a humorous side, as with the list mentioned above which reports the patron saints of various illegal activities. The following short list is used for the introduction of a character: "Era el tal medio tuerto, medio cojo, medio sordo, medio idiota y medio hermano . . . " [He was half blind, half crippled, half deaf, half idiot, and half brother . . .] (p. 177). A list of stories told by the town gossip, liar, and character assassin, Juan Pablo Longorio de la Rada, contains many stories humorously melodramatic and farfetched. The list begins:

Miren, allí va el padre Antonio Larios; todos, absolutamente todos los sermones que predica, no son de él, ¡qué van a ser de ese tontaina! . . . aquélla es la rica doña Juana Sotelo, a quien todos conocen, pero no sabe nadie, yo sí lo sé, que las noches no las pasa en su casa, en donde sólo se queda estornudando su catarro el cornalón de su marido, y ella anda en un puro retozo con el Superintendente de los Reales Azogues . . .

[Look! There goes Father Antonio Larios; all, absolutely all of the sermons he gives he didn't write. How could that idiot have produced them? . . . over there is Mrs. Juana Sotelo, a rich woman whom everyone knows, but nobody knows but me—I certainly do know—that she doesn't spend her nights at home, where her cuckold husband sits at night sneezing, while she frolicks with the Superintendant of the Treasury; . . .] (p. 243–44).

He goes on to slander many other people, dead and alive, including Sor Juana Inés de la Cruz and Carlos de Sigüenza y Góngora. These few examples of lists, many of them humorous, barely touch the surface of the lists incorporated into the book.

The use of diminutives and augmentatives constitute another linguistic source of humor in *El Canillitas*. Again, the book's title offers the first example of this device. The protagonist is so slight and bony that he cannot be compared to a regular shin bone, but a minute one. At different stages of Félix's life diminutives indicate his scanty build, such as "animalillo" [little animal] as a baby, and "nerviosillo y saltarín" [a little nervous and jumpy] as a boy. These and other diminutives function to emphasize Félix's laughably unbelievable lack of body weight. Augmentatives constitute an even more effective tool in creating humor. These simply add an exclamation point to adjectives. The word "zonzo" [fool] in itself has a comic feel, but one character is called "zonzorrión, que es zonzo en grado superlativo" [zonzorrión, which is a fool to a superlative degree] (p. 18).

Valle-Arizpe endowed *El Canillitas* with a rich supply of stylistic charm. Wit, situational and linguistic irony, comparisons, names and nicknames, lists, and suffixes all figure among the repertoire of stylistic devices used to tickle the reader's funny bone. Without a doubt, the novel both teaches its readers about Colonial Mexico and entertains them, in part through humor, as has been shown here. Thus, *El Canillitas,* in both educating and delighting its reader, follows squarely in the rich tradition of the picaresque in Mexico.

8

Hasta no verte Jesús mío

Wherein Hasta no verte Jesús mío *by Elena Poniatowska is placed within the context of both its author's literary career and tendencies of Mexican novels from its era, after which its picaresque characteristics are identified, followed by an analysis of the text's surprising, leisurely narrative pace, which creates an unusual contrast to the enormous amount of material related in the text, and generates a particularly rich portrait of the novel's picara.*

ELENA PONIATOWSKA PUBLISHED HER SECOND NOVEL, *HASTA NO verte Jesús mío* [*Until I Don't See You, Jesus*], in 1969.[1] At the time of its publication, she had established a sterling reputation as a journalist in Mexico City. She received Mexico's National Prize for Journalism in 1978, the first woman recipient of that prize.[2] Since *Hasta no verte*'s appearance, Poniatowska's literary star has continued to rise with her steady journalistic production, several books on the 1968 tragedy at Tlatelolco, several more on other themes, and a drama.[3] In fact, *La noche de Tlatelolco* [*The Night of Tlatelolco*], a collection of journalistic writings and interviews regarding the massacre, has become a basic source on the subject. In 1983 it was already in its forty-third printing. In all types of writing she has done, Poniatowska prefers to conceal or minimize her authorial presence, perhaps a reflection of her background in journalism.

According to John S. Brushwood, metafiction, Tlatelolco, life in Mexico City, matters related to identity, and nostalgia constitute the major characteristics of Mexican fiction between 1967 and 1982.[4] Three of these characteristics figure in *Hasta no verte Jesús mío,* although none plays a major role. First, many of the events in the novel take place in Mexico City. However, life in the capital yields center stage to the life of Jesusa Palancares, the novel's protagonist. Second, identity of women, men, and Mexico, especially with regard to the Revolution, comprise an underlying current in the text. Finally, history provides a very visible backdrop for much of the action of the novel. As the protagonist narrates

99

the events of her life she makes reference to historical figures such as Villa and Cárdenas, or tells of personal encounters with national figures such as Emiliano Zapata. Nostalgia often shows through her view of the past, especially since she sees the present in less than favorable terms. Thus, *Hasta no verte* shares several characteristics with other Mexican narratives of the same period.

The fact that a number of picaresque characteristics pervade Poniatowska's novel could indicate further nostalgia, in that using such elements harkens back to a cultural past. However, unlike the *Periquillo, La vida inútil de Pito Pérez,* and *El Canillitas,* the text itself does not refer to other picaresque novels. In fact, while the above-mentioned novels categorize themselves with the subgenre, *Hasta no verte* does not. The author's account of the book's creation constitutes evidence that she did not consciously conceive it as picaresque. Poniatowska states that she overheard the person Jesusa Palancares talking one day and requested an interview with her. In spite of Jesusa's initial resistance to the idea, Poniatowska did meet with her every Wednesday for two hours for the next two years to hear of her life. Poniatowska describes the transformation of the interviews into a novel:

> Utilicé las anécdotas, las ideas y muchos de los modismos de Jesusa Palancares pero no podría afirmar que es una transcripción directa de su vida. . . . Maté a los personajes que me sobraban, eliminé cuanta sesión espiritualista pude, elaboré donde me pareció necesario, podé, cosí, remendé, inventé.

> [I used the anecdotes, the ideas, and many of the turns of phrase of Jesusa Palancares but I couldn't state that it is a direct transcription of her life. . . . I killed the characters I felt were extra, I eliminated all the the spiritualist sessions possible, I elaborated when I felt it necessary, I pruned, I sewed, I patched, I invented.][5]

This description of the book's genesis brings to mind *Infortunios de Alonso Ramírez.* Like *Infortunios,* the text at hand has a curious, undeterminable relationship between author and narrator. The author listened to the oral *récit* of the narrator, then created a novel from it. Since we do not have access to transcripts from the original oral account given by the person Jesusa Palancares, we cannot know to what extent it has been transformed by Poniatowska to arrive at the *récit* we have in *Hasta no verte.* However, unlike *Infortunios,* because of the author's account of writing the narrative, *Hasta no verte* can be classified as a novel without reservation.

Hasta no verte was in its twenty-second printing in 1983. Despite the continued demand for and distribution of the book, it has garnered sparse critical comment. For the most part the book has been approached from the perspective of feminist criticism.

Joel Hancock sees the novel as "a landmark in Mexican literature because it offers a fresh view and treatment of Latin American woman, and may represent a step toward the delineation of a new female image or role model."[6] Using Jungian psychology, Monique Lemaitre seconds the motion for Jesusa Palancares representing a new type of Mexican woman.[7] Edward H. Friedman focuses on ironies in the text that stem from the differing perspectives of the narrator and the implied author.[8] He sees Palancares' act of narrating the novel as liberating for her, giving her a chance to develop her personality. Experts of the picaresque have made similar statements regarding classic picaros.

Let us now turn to the picaresque elements in *Hasta no verte Jesús mío*.

1) *Episodic Plot.* Episodes do indeed drive the structure of Poniatowska's novel. Experiences from Jesusa's life, most of them independent of one another, frame the tale with the protagonist serving as its only sustained element. Although various characters appear in more than one chapter, such as Jesusa's father in chapters two through seven (of twenty-nine), the overall structure remains episodic.

2) *Dizzying Rhythm.* The pace of *Hasta no verte* is unexpectedly subdued and far from vertiginous. This element of the text receives extended analysis later in this chapter.

3) *Fate Rules Supreme.* Fate as such never surfaces overtly in the book. However, Jesusa's religious beliefs serve much the same function as fate. Jesusa resigns herself to a life of suffering because she believes God controls all and that she is doing penance for her unrighteousness in previous lives. However, unlike other picaresque novels in which strokes of bad luck at key moments prohibit the picaro from enjoying a newfound prosperity, bad luck does not victimize Jesusa in *Hasta no verte.* Rather, she sees her life as one of prescribed misfortune.

4) *Bodily Violence.* During the first third of the novel, when Jesusa's family relationships dominate the text, violence surfaces regularly. She sees her brother beat his wife with regularity; her sister suffers abuse over the course of several years and finally dies of fright after her husband makes an attempt

on her life. Jesusa also suffers occasional abuses. Her stepmother in particular torments her, giving her frequent beatings. Ironically, Jesusa harbors no resentment toward her stepmother, instead remembering her as the person who taught her valuable life lessons. By contrast, she resents the senseless punishment she receives from her husband. Finally one day when Pedro takes her out to beat her, she pulls a gun on him. Starting at that moment Jesusa avoids further physical abuse from Pedro or anyone else.

5a) *A Single Protagonist.* As the novel's only possible protagonist, the title *The Life of Jesusa Palancares* would accurately reflect its content.

5b) *Uncommon Origins.* Jesusa's mother died before she turned six, and did little to prepare her daughter for life. Jesusa's father, although never affectionate or nurturing with his children, did accept the responsibility of providing for and taking care of them. However, when the children were young and without anyone to care for them, while at work he would lock them in a shack, even on dangerously hot days. When he realized his work made it impossible to care for his family properly, he would leave their care to acquaintances or stepmothers. In these situations Jesusa received very little training and even less love. Eventually, before Jesusa's fifteenth birthday, her father rejected her, died soon thereafter, and she became an orphan.

5c) *Cunning.* At one point a drunkard makes unsolicited sexual advances to Jesusa. She reacts to his overtures by thrashing him violently with a stick. She realizes the police will come looking for her, so she hurries home, changes her clothes, and combs her hair. When the police arrive with the victim of her assault, he cannot recognize her and she avoids a trip to jail. This anecdote illustrates Jesusa's capacity for cunning, but she rarely exercises it. Although not entirely absent from the text, the protagonist survives thanks to hard work rather than trickery.

5d) *Protean Form.* Jesusa boasts a formidable list of professions in which she has worked during her long lifetime: assistant in a pharmacy, nanny, cook, soldier, commander, factory worker, launderer, dancer, waitress, nurse, butcher, maid, and businessperson. Her constant shift from one job to another evidences both her resistance to confining situations and her ability to adapt to new roles and responsibilities.

5e) *Alienation.* In his study on *Hasta no verte,* Edward Friedman emphasizes the silence imposed on Jesusa's life before she narrates the novel. People rarely talk to her, and she has even fewer opportunities to talk. Of course, alienation constitutes one side effect of her silence. Jesusa can hardly feel that she has any solidarity with her fellow beings when she cannot communicate with them. At one point she claims that the only person she ever loved was her brother. Such a statement implies an absence of love in all her other family relationships, especially in her marriage. Although she has occasional fraternal friendships, they come only rarely and end quickly. She usually faces life alone. Her lack of identification with other people even keeps her from experiencing feelings of nationalism.

5f) *Internal Instability.* Jesusa's ornery disposition leads her often into fights and fits of rage that would seem to indicate a lack of interior stability. However, when she fights, she does so thanks to a firm internal resolve to maintain her independence and do what is proper. On several occasions she raises other people's children out of a sense of duty. She recognizes herself that she has great resolve and willpower, far surpassing that of the average picaro.

5g) *A Philosophical Bent.* Jesusa voices strong philosophical leanings throughout the text. Jesusa expresses opinions on Mexico, men, death, fighting, unions, government, the revolution, vices, homosexuality, doctors, the military, etc. Her observations go beyond the world around her, for her intense involvement with a spiritualist religious group leads her to have strong views on such subjects as reincarnation, communication with the dead, and overall views of life. In short, Jesusa joins Pito Pérez as a sort of philosopher of the common people.

6) *The First-person Point of View. Hasta no verte* follows in the tradition of classic picaresque novels in its first-person narrative point of view. Jesusa Palancares tells her own life story retrospectively; thus, she plays the dual role of protagonist and narrator. The difference between her narrating self and experiencing self at times becomes very obvious, highlighted by temporal shifts from past to present. In both modes the point of view remains first-person.

7) *An Unkind, Chaotic World.* Jesusa obviously does not belong to Mexico's upper or middle classes. She is a poor, exploited laborer in a bleak world. Nevertheless, the chaotic world in which she lives receives little emphasis in the text, such as in

the description of the hospital for women suffering from venereal diseases. Chaotic and unkind certainly describe Jesusa's world, but the text spotlights Jesusa's bleak life instead.

8)   *Physical Survival.* Hunger and depravation definitely surface in Jesusa's life from time to time. However, when she misses meals, she merely tries to convince herself that she is not hungry. As a reaction to the times of hunger, Jesusa often spends extra time telling of the details of meals during more abundant times. Similarly, since she knows homelessness, she often makes special mention of places of shelter she enjoys during happier times. In short, the text does give special attention to Jesusa's physical needs.

9)   *A Vast Gallery of Human Types.* The extensive cast of supporting characters in Jesusa's life comprises well-rounded characters rather than caricatures or stereotypes. Certainly some of the characters could represent a certain type of people, for example, Felipe exemplifies the unaffectionate but dutiful father, Pedro Aguilar typifies the wife-beating, macho husband, and Evarista epitomizes the demanding, cruel stepmother. Yet these characters have very human traits, many of which do not correspond to "their type." Rather than a vast gallery of human types, humans seem to populate the vast gallery in *Hasta no verte.*

The entirety of *Hasta no verte Jesús mío* contains an abundance of basic story material. In broad terms, Jesusa tells the story of her long and eventful life, which spans more than seventy years, in more than three hundred pages. Curiously, in spite of the numerous events spanning many years, the pace of the narrative seems unhurried. The remainder of this chapter explores the nature of the book's seemingly leisurely narrative pace.

To facilitate the study of this phenomenon I make use of Gerard Genette's terminology relative to narrative pace:

> . . . scene takes the same amount of time in the récit and the histoire. Summary takes less time in the récit than in the histoire. Descriptive pause takes up immeasurably (incapable of being measured) more time in the récit than in the histoire. Ellipse takes up immeasurably less time in the récit than in the histoire.[9]

Most of the pauses in *Hasta no verte Jesús mío* are not descriptive in nature but analytical. The narrator refrains from carrying forward the action of the narration, but instead comments on it. This study refers to such a phenomenon as "analytical pause." Analytical pause describes the same phenomenon as descriptive pause in terms of the relationship between *récit* and *histoire*.

To keep this analysis succinct, we examine the pace of only one of *Hasta no verte*'s twenty-nine chapters. Some chapters narrate more events than others. I have chosen an event-rich chapter since it focuses on Jesusa's involvement in the Revolution. I have numbered the lines in the chapter in the following table to aid in referring to specific sections of it.

Page	Lines	Page	Lines
103	1–34	108	198–38
104	35–74	109	239–79
105	75–15	110	280–20
106	116–56	111	321–58
107	157–97	112	359–69

The chapter begins with a brief paragraph that acts as a type of topic statement for the chapter: "Mi marido tenía una suerte de perro amarillo con las mujeres. Lo seguían mucho y cuando no les hacía caso se valían de trasmano para ponerme en mal." [My husband was unusually lucky with women. They followed him all over and when he would pay them no attention they went out of their way to take it out on me] (lines 1–3, p. 103). The first sentence is a brief analytical pause, while the second is more difficult to classify. A case could be made for either summary or a type of ellipse. Technically, the sentence is a summary, since a chain of events is being related. However, use of the imperfect tense complicates the matter. Its use indicates that the events occurred an undisclosed number of times in the past.[10] Thus, the *récit* takes immeasurably (incapable of being measured) less time than the *histoire*—the definition of ellipse. Just as with pauses, whether descriptive or analytical, with iterative summary the *récit* overrules the passing of time in the *histoire*. An accurate sense of time in the *histoire* becomes impossible because the events of the story slow or stand still. Likewise, the narrative pace retards or comes to a halt.

The next portion of the chapter (lines 4–78, pp. 103–5) tells the story of Angelita, the only one of Pedro's lovers whom Jesusa meets personally. The second paragraph of the chapter consists purely of summary (lines 4–15, p. 103). Jesusa relates that she knows Pedro has a lover by the name of Angelita, and that after Angelita's husband confronts Pedro over their relationship, Pedro batters him and ends up in jail. When Jesusa goes to visit her husband and take him some food, she finds Angelita there also.

Summary then gives way to scene (lines 16–23, p. 103) and we witness the brief conversation that takes place in the jail. Jesusa berates the couple with regard to their relationship, while Pedro counters with an inane denial. Summary again returns (lines 24–35, pp. 103–4) as Jesusa tells that she leaves the jail with no small amount of indignation. She sees Angelita run home, so Jesusa follows her for a confrontation. A short scene (lines 36–38, p. 104) shows Jesusa's inquiry for Angelita at the door with the owner of the house. Two lines of summary (39–40, p. 104), in which the owner identifies Angelita, precede an utterance by the owner directed to her boarder: "¡Sáquese! Yo no admito pleitos en mi casa" [Get out! I don't allow fights in my house] (scene, line 41, p. 104).

The narrator uses summary to describe the ensuing confrontation (lines 42–54, p. 104). Despite Angelita's attempts to flee, Jesusa catches her, fights with her, disfigures her, and then allows her to run home to her husband. A short scene shows us the verbal reaction of Angelina's husband to her arrival (lines 55–56, p. 104). He tells her she deserves the punishment Jesusa gave her and tells her to leave. The next few lines of the text interrupt the *histoire*'s chronology of events (lines 57–68, p. 104). As a group, these lines function as a narrative pause, even though on the surface they seem a continuation of scene and summary. The summary in lines 57–58 and scene in lines 59–61 relate what Jesusa heard about Angelita at a later date—that her face was permanently scarred. Pure descriptive pause occurs in lines 62–63 as Jesusa describes Angelita's physical beauty before their fight. This triggers a line of iterative summary (line 64, p. 104) followed by a scene (lines 65–67, p. 104) and then another line of iterative summary (68, p. 104). In these lines Jesusa relates that when she used to fight with Pedro (once again, an undeterminable number of times) she would tell him at least to cheat with beautiful women. Thus, lines 57–68 do not carry the basic story forward but expand on it and digress from it, effectively pausing the narrative pace.

We return briefly to the story line as Jesusa relates Pedro's lack of response to her actions with Angelita (summary, lines 69–72, p. 104). Without even switching to a new paragraph, a section which functions as analytical pause begins disguised as iterative summary (lines 72–91, pp. 104–5). Clearly a spinoff from the narration of Pedro's relationship with Angelita, this section has Jesusa clearing Pedro of any responsibility for his relationships with other women since they pursue him, not vice versa. Even in lines 77–79, in which Jesusa backtracks to tell how Angelita went after Pedro, what seems to be summary actually functions as a pause. Likewise,

what appears to be scene in lines 82–83 also functions within the
framework of a pause: "Por eso digo que como hombre no le que-
daba más remedio que cumplirles. ¿Qué hacía Pedro si se le iban
a ofrecer? ¿Decirles: 'Vete, no te quiero?'" [That's why I say that
as a man he had no other choice but to comply. What was Pedro
to do if they went to him offering themselves? Tell them, "Go
away I don't want you?"] (p. 105). The following summarizes the
narrative pace of the chapter's first eighty-three lines:

1	Analytical Pause
2–3	Ellipse (Summary in imperfect tense)
4–15	Summary
16–23	Scene
24–35	Summary
36–38	Scene
39–40	Summary
41	Scene
42–54	Summary
55–56	Scene
57–68	Pause

       57–58   Summary
       59–61   Scene
       62–63   Descriptive Pause
       64–68   Iterative Summary
             64   Iterative Summary
          65–67   Scene
             68   Iterative Summary

69–72	Summary
72–91	Analytical Pause

       72–76   Analytical Pause
       77–79   Summary
       80–81   Analytical Pause
       82–83   Scene
       84–91   Analytical Pause

Another anecdote begins on line 92, thus implying an ellipse even
though no overt temporal markers exist. Still on the theme of
women in Pedro's life, this time Jesusa tells of overhearing that
another woman is pursuing Pedro. She decides not to confront

either Pedro or the woman. The pattern of narration parallels that of the chapter's first anecdote:

92–94	Summary
95–96	Scene
97–00	Summary
101–13	Analytical Pause
101–7	Analytical & Descriptive Pause
108–11	Iterative Scene
112–13	Iterative Summary

As with the chapter's first anecdote, summary dominates this one, but scene adds further color to the story. When she finishes the actual anecdote, the narrator pauses to analyze the story she has just told, draw conclusions, and back up her conclusions through further illustrations.

After another implied ellipse, she tells a new anecdote. Unlike the first two of the chapter, neither descriptive nor analytical pause interrupts this anecdote, in which someone poisons her husband. We hear of Pedro's physical reaction to the poison and the curious treatment he receives from a *curandero*. The narrator tells the story with the following mixture of scene and summary:

114–24	Summary
125	Scene
126–33	Summary
134–36	Scene
137–38	Summary
139–46	Scene
147–49	Summary
150–56	Scene

Rather than again launching into an analytical mode, the narrator instead tells another anecdote. This time she lays bare the transitional ellipse: "Después de su accidente mi marido hasta me llevaba a la calle y un día cuando íbamos al mandado, oí . . . " [After his accident my husband even took me out to the street and one day when we were on our way to run errands, I heard . . .] (p. 107). Once again this episode deals with Jesusa's husband's relationships with other women. We see Pedro here banning a woman, presumably formerly one of his lovers, from his presence. He threatens her with violence and finally has his right-hand man put her on a train and send her away. The anecdote is narrated in the following way:

157–59	Summary
160	Scene
161–62	Summary
163–77	Scene
178	Summary
179–80	Scene
181–82	Summary
183	Scene
184–85	Summary
186–327	Pause (primarily analytical, with some iterative scene and summary)

The lengthy pause at the story's conclusion begins with a physical description of the woman Pedro has his man put on the train. It continues with a brief comment on her background. The narrator then gives her opinion on extramarital relationships and goes on to discuss, among other things, how many women Pedro had during the revolution, her rocky relationship with Pedro, how she would treat him, and her duties, feelings, and activities during the revolution. Whereas historical accounts generally focus on the series of events in a war, the narrator of *Hasta no verte* instead refers to Mexico's revolution in terms of the conditions, relationships, and feelings she experienced. In a section we would expect to be rapid-paced with an abundance of scene and summary, analytical pause reigns instead, bringing along with it a pace far from frenzied.

Near the end of Jesusa's ramblings during the lengthy analytical pause mentioned above, she speaks of inclement weather during the revolution. This leads to weather-related stories from that time period. She relates the first in pure summary, telling the effects of a heavy rainstorm (lines 328–40, p. 111). The company gets so muddy that the women have to wash its clothing, which is stolen when hung out to dry.

Four spaces separate lines 340 and 341. These spaces may indicate a space of time between interview sessions. They also seem to imply an ellipse, although once again we do not know the chronology of the *récit* compared to the *histoire*. Jesusa continues to discuss weather during the revolution, but this time snow, and the protagonist's reaction to it, enjoy the text's center stage. With the exception of the use of a brief scene (lines 362–63, p. 112), in the remainder of the chapter (lines 341–69, pp. 111–112) summary marks the narration. The imperfect tense dominates this section; however, the action seems to go forward much more than in earlier sections using iterative summary. Nonetheless, the pace of the narrative slows by using imperfect rather than preterite.

The following chart numerically presents the use of summary, scene, and pause in chapter ten:

Anecdote:	Pre	1	2	3	4	5	6	TOTAL
Summary:	2	43	7	25	10	13	29	129
Scene:	—	14	2	19	19	—	2	56
Pause:	1	32	13	—	142	—	—	188

Overall, the chapter utilizes far more pause than summary or scene. In fact, it uses more pause than summary and scene combined. By looking strictly at these statistics, we see that the pace of the narrative can hardly be called dizzying. Let us also remember the iterative nature of some of the chapter's summary, which also slows the pace of the narrative. Furthermore, because the chronological relationship between anecdotes becomes clear in only one instance, the implied ellipse between the others communicates the sense that the events of the protagonist's life never bear down on her in rapid succession.

The findings of the foregoing paragraph apply to all of *Hasta no verte,* especially because this study analyzes a more action-based chapter than most in the book. Thus, pause undoubtedly dominates over scene and summary to an even greater extent in the entire book than it does in chapter ten. The pattern of telling an anecdote with a mixture of scene and summary followed by large doses of analytical pause extends throughout the text. Just as in this chapter, chronological relationships between anecdotes typically remain undefined throughout the text. Also, summary features frequent use of the imperfect tense throughout the text, just as we saw in chapter 10. All these factors account for the subdued pace of the narrative.

The book's less-than-dizzying pace affects its readers in significant ways. Rather than traveling quickly with the protagonist from episode to episode in the past, readers instead spend most of their time with the narrator in the present. Rather than appeal to readers looking for an action-based narrative, Poniatowska's novel instead appeals to readers interested in getting to know the thoughts, opinions, and feelings of the character/narrator Jesusa Palancares. The narrative pace indicates that in *Hasta no verte Jesús mío* the implied author concerns herself less with the life events of a picara than with the picara herself.

9

El Chanfalla

Wherein El Chanfalla, *by Gonzalo Martré, is found to be representative of novels of its time period, after which its abundant picaresque characteristics are identified and discussed, following which it is shown that episodes in the text which show the unreliability of appearances and others that contain fantastic elements, joined by the narrator's highly contrived style of narration, all join to encourage readers to delve more deeply into the sticky relationship between appearance and reality.*

SINCE THE PUBLICATION OF *HASTA NO VERTE JESÚS MÍO,* a number of narratives have been published that contain prominent picaresque characteristics. *El Chanfalla,* published by Gonzalo Martré in 1979, incorporates the greatest number.[1] According to the novel's jacket, Martré has written narratives of two types: socioerotic (a term coined by the author) and political. It further classifies *El Chanfalla* as a political novel and states that it constitutes the first volume of a tetralogy, although to date the subsequent volumes have not been published. It deals principally with the decade of the 1930s.

According to John Brushwood, metafiction, Tlatelolco, life in Mexico City, exploration of identity, and nostalgia constitute the major characteristics of Mexican fiction between 1967 and 1982.[2] The same three elements found in *Hasta no verte Jesús mío* make up the fabric of *El Chanfalla;* however, these elements differ greatly in the two novels. Although both novelists set their novels in Mexico City, it stays in the background in Poniatowska's novel, while life in the capital is the essence of Martré's. It thoroughly describes and illustrates the professions, living conditions, attitudes, and social relationships of the lower classes in Mexico City. Identity plays a major thematic role in Martré's narrative. However, unlike *Hasta no verte Jesús mío,* in which the emphasis on identity focuses on the protagonist, *El Chanfalla* places the spotlight of identity on the masses of lower- and working-class people. Readers see how national politics and labor movements of the thirties affected common people. "Nostalgia" may not entirely describe the way in which the text turns to the past, since a great deal of the subject matter is unpleasant and unattractive. However, at least a form of nostalgia presents itself in returning to the Cárdenas era. In sum, although it is devoid of metafiction and reference to Tlatelolco, *El Chanfalla* includes considerations dealing with life in Mexico City, identity, and a small dose of nostalgia. Thus, it does not depart radically from the mainstream of Mexican fiction of its era.

Regarding its relationship to the picaresque family, only the book's jacket mentions the subgenre. Like *Hasta no verte Jesús mío,* and in contrast to *La vida inútil de Pito Pérez* and *El Canillitas,* the text itself of *El Chanfalla* seems unaware of its picaresque kinship. Rather than attempting to write a picaresque novel, using a young boy merely as a vehicle, the implied author seems to have set out to write a novel about Mexico City in the thirties. The picaresque product seems to be a coincidental result.

Three critics have written on *El Chanfalla.* In a review that deals primarily with the issue of the work's relationship to the picaresque subgenre, Ignacio Trejo Fuentes places the novel only partially in the picaresque family.[3] He lauds the novel's storytelling and definition of characters. Wolfgang A. Luchting objects to the book's use of fantastic elements and long passages dealing with history, but recognizes it as an entertaining work.[4] John Brushwood lauds the novel's technique, since the picaresque has traditionally been used to criticize society.[5]

We now turn to a discussion of the narrative's picaresque characteristics.

1) *Episodic Plot.* Although episodic describes *El Chanfalla*'s plot, it differs from the other narratives previously examined. In this book, characters other than the picaro often appear in more than one episode of the text. Some members of Chanfalla's supporting cast appear in numerous chapters throughout the novel. Nevertheless, although the protagonist does not provide the only link between episodes, he constitutes its only major link. The other recurring characters appear only occasionally in the text, but their development remains stunted, and their relationship with Chanfalla never becomes significantly intimate or dynamic.

   El Chanfalla's plot also differs from the classic picaresque notion in its nonlinear chronology. The first fifteen of the book's thirty-five chapters alternate between the book's main story line and flashbacks to episodes in the picaro's life. More specifically, chapters 1, 3, 5, 7, 9, 11, 12, 14, and 16 through 35 tell the essence of the story. Chapter two tells of the picaro's parents obtaining his birth certificate; four describes the details of his baptism; six relates his serious childhood illness; and so forth. Thus, although the novel's plot differs technically in several ways from most picaresque texts, its essence remains entirely episodic.

2) *Dizzying Rhythm. El Chanfalla*'s pace hurries along, especially after the first fifteen chapters, when flashbacks stop interrupting the main story line. Both picaro and reader experience numerous episodes and situations at a very rapid clip, which bedazzles both.

3) *Fate Rules Supreme.* Late in the novel, speaking of the picaro the narrator states: "Aceptaba los hechos tal y como se presentaban, sujeto al determinismo que regía su vida" [He accepted the events as they happened to him, subject to the determinism that ruled his life] (p. 246). Certainly the picaro acts as a mere pawn in a dreadful situation. Chanfalla's legal names illustrate his powerlessness. When his parents take him to the authorities as a baby, the capricious official, who tells his assistant that he feels very patriotic that day, ignores the illiterate parents' request to name their son Ulogio Guerrero Ortíz, and instead names him Agustín de Iturbide y Guerrero. Although he often works hard and more often uses his cunning, he does not escape his vagabond existence until the novel's end, when returning to his family looks possible. However, even if he succeeds he will remain in the lower class. Thus, throughout the text, although he scores minor victories, Chanfalla stands defenseless in his overall battle with fate.

4) *Bodily Violence.* Although not emphasized in the narrative, violence forms part of our picaro's world, and on occasion it strikes him. Before leaving home the neighborhood bully shows him no mercy. In fact, Chanfalla abandons his home because when he finally retaliates, he thinks he has killed his adversary and fears going to jail. Out on his own he witnesses fatal traffic accidents, beatings, and torture. On one occasion police beat him, and two other times strangers do the same. Indeed, bodily violence exists with a vengeance in Chanfalla's world.

5a) *A Single Protagonist.* Agustín de Iturbide y Guerrero, better known by his nickname, Chanfalla, constitutes the novel's only possible protagonist. Appropriately, one of the picaros in Cervantes' short drama, *El retablo de las maravillas,* has the name Chanfalla.

5b) *Uncommon Origins.* Chanfalla is not the typical picaresque orphan, nor did his parents physically abandon him. Rather, Chanfalla abandoned them. Nevertheless, his home life gives no evidence of family nurturing or even communication. At a very young age he might as well be an orphan because he has to fend for himself on the street rather than enjoying protection from loving parents. Little changes after he leaves home, except that he lacks a regular place to sleep. Thus, although not an orphan, Chanfalla's origins seem an appropriate starting point for a life of chaos.

5c) *Cunning.* The first evidence of Chanfalla's capacity for cunning comes before he leaves home. A friend requests his help in arranging for his girlfriend to escape from the control of her unsympathetic father so they can elope. Chanfalla cleverly, surreptitiously carries notes for the couple, smuggles her clothing out of the house, and distracts the father at the moment of truth. Without his cunning, the protagonist would not survive the challenges of street life in the city. Perhaps the most entertaining instance of Chanfalla's craftiness comes after an upper-class woman wanders into the poor part of town and loses her purse. The police round up all the rogues in the area and ask the woman to identify the culprit. Although completely innocent, Chanfalla thinks the woman is paying too much attention to him. Rather than risk being charged for someone else's crime, he feigns an epileptic seizure with such skill that authorities take him for medical treatment instead.

5d) *Protean Form.* The list of professions practiced by Chanfalla is astounding in light of the fact that at the text's end he is not even thirteen years of age. The activity in which he engages most often is that of *vendedor ambulante* [street salesperson]. The list of items he sells at different stages is impressive: coal, newspapers, balloons, sweet potatoes and bananas, *banderillas* near a bullring, ice cream bars, fruit, *merengues* [a type of dessert], and *buñuelos* [a type of fritter]. Other professions in which he works include rat hunter (he sells them to the meat shop), singer on buses, fire-eater, clown, announcer for a circus, thief, gambler, assistant to a barber, assistant in a gypsy-bear street show, assistant to an herb healer, and assistant to a magician. Chanfalla exhibits a remarkable capacity to function in a variety of professions, and thus demonstrates unmistakable Protean form.

5e) *Alienation.* As mentioned above, Chanfalla's family does not provide him with nurturing or love. A neighbor of Chanfalla's family, Don Pedro Rendón, a poet and artist, begins and ends the list of characters in the novel who treat him with affection. Unfortunately, Rendón has minimal contact with Chanfalla. His relationship with almost everyone else in the novel is strictly businesslike. If characters hold an interest in him, they typically do so hoping to exploit him as a mere resource. His life so lacks love and affection that he spends much of his time at the movies, "único remedio contra la melancolía" [his only recourse against melancholy] (p. 146). In the book's penultimate chapter he falls in love with Agustina, who responds to his love. However, they soon become bitter enemies. Chanfalla suffers almost complete alienation from his world.

5f) *Internal Instability.* Although he constantly switches jobs, and comes from a chaotic family, Chanfalla achieves a remarkable degree of internal stability. He tries to stay within the law and almost always succeeds. His penchant for spending or gambling away his earnings as quickly as he makes them results more from his training than from an internal flaw. On several occasions he overcomes the treatment he has received to show compassion to others. He rarely participates in practical jokes and capriciousness. Although not a pillar of consistency, I see Chanfalla not as an example of a person suffering from internal instability, but as a fairly responsible ten-year-old.

5g) *A Philosophical Bent.* Chanfalla's obsessive interest in national politics and the workers' movements seems very unnatural for a young boy. Frankly, the protagonist's philosophical bent seems artificial and pedantic.

6) *The First-person Point of View. El Chanfalla* makes use of a third-person rather than a first-person narrative point of view. Its past tense only occasionally finds focalization through Chanfalla. This point of view and the narrator's preference for presenting aspects of Mexico City's life lead to a somewhat superficial depiction of the picaro.

7) *An Unkind, Chaotic World.* As already noted, *El Chanfalla's* representation of Mexico City in the 1930s constitutes one of its greatest strengths. The narrator describes in great detail the unpleasant, degrading, agitated living conditions of the

city's lower classes during the Cárdenas era. The unpleasant conditions in the city lead to self-interested and sometimes hostile behavior among the people. Confidence men crop up, law officials go corrupt, crime spreads, and people gather into sometimes dangerous groups to multiply their survival capabilities. Thus, the world in which Chanfalla lives can indeed be called both unkind and chaotic.

8) *Physical Survival.* Chanfalla's constant drive to provide for his own basic shelter and sustenance is implied throughout most of the narrative, even though it is rarely overtly expressed. Through his industriousness, he rarely endures hunger, but he knows exposure to the elements, as is seen in this passage:

> Como era invierno buscó techo sin hallarlo, como cama tuvo el quicio de los zaguanes, como almohada ladrillos, como colchón cartones, como frazada papeles rescatados de la basura, durmió a la intemperie en los barrios humildes . . .

> [Since it was winter he sought shelter, but unsuccessfully; for a bed he used an outside passageway, bricks were his pillow, cardboard his cushion, papers from garbage cans his blankets; he slept at the mercy of the elements in the most humble parts of town . . .] (p. 86).

Physical survival forms a strong undercurrent to much of the text.

9) *A Vast Gallery of Human Types.* A good number and variety of human types cross Chanfalla's path in the course of the novel. Some of the notable characters in the text include Popocha, the omnipresent policeman who is a law unto himself; "Drácula," the young Don Juan of Chanfalla's neighborhood; Lalo, who bullies Chanfalla but also serves as the punching bag of the Hormiga brothers; Licerciado Joachim, the justice of the peace who whimsically chooses names for the babies of illiterate parents; Tonelillo, the eight-year-old leader of a ring of thieves; Lucha la Carbonera, who begins by selling coal and ends up selling everything from pastries to marijuana; Martín de la Cruz, the bogus salesman of herbs for every ailment; Richard Rasec, a sleight-of-hand expert and fakir; Beto el Cilindrero, who feigns blindness to garner sympathy and alms; and Father Nicomedes, the money-hungry priest. Curious cameo appearances are even made by several real-life people from the era. For example, Chanfalla poses

for Diego Rivera as he paints the mural in the stairway of the national palace. The real-life silver-tongued labor leader Lombardo Toledano mesmerizes Chanfalla with a speech. The cast of characters in *El Chanfalla* is indeed rich and entertaining.

El Chanfalla posits the issue of identity as one of its central concerns. The text explores the identities of Mexico, Mexico City, the labor movement, politics, politicians, and individuals. It intertwines the issues of reality and identity. Early in Chanfalla's life, he receives a poorly made wooden truck for Christmas, along with a disclaimer that the three kings are still poor, as they have been in the past. On the recommendation of Lalo, Chanfalla travels to a rich neighborhood to see the Christmas gifts there. This adventure results in the shocking discovery that it wasn't the three kings (the Mexican equivalent of Santa Claus) who were poor, but the parents of poor children. Chanfalla learns the lesson early in life that things are not always what they seem, and that one must be active in ascertaining what is real and what is illusion. The implied author uses a number of strategies that point readers to the same lesson. The remainder of this chapter explores ways in which the implied author leads his readers to see the unreliable nature of perceived reality, challenges them to seek to go beyond appearances, and provides them with heightened awareness thereof.

The most transparent method the implied author uses to point his readers to the issue of reality appears in the anecdote cited in the preceding paragraph. Many of the episodes in the text exemplify the discrepancies that often exist between appearance and reality. Examples are numerous, and in many of them, Chanfalla has an active role in producing misleading appearances. As assistant to Richard Rasec, the sleight-of-hand expert, Chanfalla finds out that his master's acts are mere tricks—appearances masquerading as reality. When Chanfalla sells *buñuelos* for Lucha la Carbonera in a graveyard on All Souls' Day, he actually acts as a front for Lucha's true business dealings—the sale of marijuana. When he sells fruit for his gang of delinquents, he is really taking note of expensive tires for the gang to steal. Thus, Chanfalla is personally involved in a number of jobs in which appearance and reality do not coincide, as is the case in many picaresque tales.

Chanfalla participates in producing illusions, and he witnesses the slippery nature of appearances on many occasions as well. His business of selling gum on buses goes well for him until a pickpocket gets on the same bus. When a victim of the thief makes a scene over her missing wallet, the culprit manipulates appearances by planting the stolen wallet at the feet of Chanfalla, who takes the rap for the crime. In their wanderings through Mexico City's downtown, Don Pedro Rendón tells Chanfalla that justice does not exist in Mexico. When the boy questions the need for a lavish palace of justice, Rendón simply answers "Para guardar las apariencias, hijito" [To protect appearances, my boy] (p. 38). Chanfalla further sees the falseness of public life when he witnesses the fraudulent election of Avila Camacho. Chanfalla's herb-selling master often knowingly sells his wares to customers with greatly exaggerated or false promises. However, on one occasion he acts with integrity and is subsequently falsely accused, beaten, and thrown in jail. The picaro's reaction to the event is logical: "La mentira, concluyó Chanfalla, es preferible a la verdad. Al que miente no puede irle mal en la vida" [Lies, concluded Chanfalla, are preferible to truth. The person who lies has an easier time in life] (p. 116). Thus, through narration of many episodes, readers are shown the unreliability of appearances as well as the danger of reality.

During the last half of the book, events occur which depart from normal associations with reality. The first of these events occurs in conjunction with Chanfalla's time as assistant to the "gypsy" (a gypsy in appearance only) and his dancing bear, Kino. Chanfalla has a strong desire to befriend Kino, and once he gets close enough, starts to talk to him. When Kino responds and a very human conversation ensues, Chanfalla reacts calmly because he has heard parrots talk before. Chanfalla and Kino converse about working conditions and even of Lombardo Toledano, whom Chanfalla heard speak on Mexico's labor movement.

In a later episode, Chanfalla makes friends with three dogs, who he nicknames Churchill, Stalin, and Roosevelt, perhaps a twist on Cervantes' *El coloquio de los perros* [*The Conversation of Dogs*]. When Stalin starts a conversation with Chanfalla, he remains unsurprised, but wonders whether anyone else can hear the dogs talk. He asks the only person within hearing distance, Don Toño Arciniegas, if he heard the dogs talk. Arciniegas suggests that he clean his ears, and Chanfalla realizes that he is the only human being able to understand the dogs. He later communicates with other dogs in the same way.

In a similar episode, an unusual man pursues Chanfalla relentlessly:

El jinete, armadura negra y bruñida, visera calada, yelmo dorado, lanza en ristre, arreos y aparejos de lujo, suceso sobrecogedor, no llamaba la atención de los peatones ni parecía estorbar el tránsito.

[The horseman, donning black, polished armor, lowered visor, golden helmet, a lance in its socket, his horse outfitted with complete trappings and riding gear, an astonishing sight, didn't catch the eye of pedestrians and didn't seem to alter traffic patterns] (p. 148)

This man reminds Chanfalla of a horseman from a Cecil B. deMille film he has seen. Later he sees Zurburán's painting of St. George subduing the dragon and concludes that St. George has been following him to punish him for Lalo's death. His acquaintances consider him either imaginative or possessed, and the horseman eventually stops following him.

The foregoing episodes, which feature fantastic elements, appear in the text as reality. If these episodes were merely focalized through Chanfalla, they could be explained as products of a vivid imagination. His loneliness and the unpleasant nature of his world drive him not only to the fantasy of the movie theater, but to the invention of his own personal fantastic reality. Nevertheless, a later episode cannot be explained so easily. When he sells ice cream bars, Chanfalla witnesses a reenactment of the events leading up to Christ's crucifixion. As he watches a man struggle under the weight of a cross, he has compassion for the man and gives him several ice cream bars. Chanfalla subsequently discovers that his box of ice cream bars cannot be depleted. Miraculously, for many days he does not have to return to the ice cream factory to replenish his stock. However, when he capriciously inflicts pain on a cat, he discovers that a row of ice cream bars has disappeared. When he kicks a dog for no particular reason, another row disappears. Just as miraculously as his supply had replenished itself, it disappears row by row as he commits unkind, cruel acts until his box is empty. This miracle cannot be a mere figment of Chanfalla's imagination, for he lives on the proceeds thereof for many days. This episode suggests that we may need to look again at the prior episodes of fantastic occurrences to reconsider whether they are imagined or real. Rather than showing evidence of Chanfalla's psychological state, these episodes as a whole seem to tell implied readers that reality is difficult, if not impossible, to grasp fully. They assert the existence of realities beyond our normal range of perception and challenge readers to go beyond appearances.

The literary style of *El Chanfalla* has a bearing on the subject of reality in a subtle, indirect way. Dialogue in the text is linguistically accurate and unadorned, reflecting the lower class, uneducated, spontaneous talk of children and other speakers. "*Onde*" instead of "Donde" [where], "*Ansina*" instead of "Así" [thus], and "*De gratis*" instead of "gratis" [free of charge] are examples of non-standard Spanish terms found just on page 172 of the text. Colloquialisms and phonetic peculiarities also lace the novel's pages. As characters speak, the narrator does not intervene and each locution is succinct and unornamented.

By contrast, the novel's passages delivered by the narrator are conspicuously correct, educated, and ornamented. A short sample here suffices:

> En su peregrinar con el filantrópico botánico, Chanfalla conoció una extensa gama de caballeros de industria y no pocos le ofrecieron empleo, rehusado debido a su fidelidad al terapeuta . . .

> [In his pilgrimage with the philanathropic botanist, Chanfalla met an extensive range of gentlemen of industry, not a few of whom offered him employment, all of which he refused due to his loyalty to the therapeutist . . .] (p. 116).

The stark contrast between dialogue and narration bombards readers with two vastly different levels of linguistic reality—one a choppy, untutored, simple form of expression, while the other is cultured, eloquent, and complex.

Because of space limitations, no extremely lengthy sentences have been included here; however, absent even from the above short selection is a single, simple, short sentence. In each case the nuclear element of the sentence is clarified, modified, or expanded. Thus, sentence structure is convoluted and complex.

The linguistic register in the above selection and throughout the book is very high. References to the herb healer alone illustrate this point. Not only is he referred to by his name, Martín de la Cruz, but also as a "filantrópico botánico" [philanthropic botanist], a "terapeuta" [therapeutist], and later a "teratológico anciano" [teratological old man]. These terms obviously overstate and unduly exalt de la Cruz. He merely sells herbs, often promising results that he knows go far beyond the capabilities of his products. The resulting irony once again points readers to the issue of reality. The discrepancy between de la Cruz's actions and the terms employed by the narrator lead us to see a gap between reality and artifice, in this case linguistic artifice.

The exalted linguistic register employed by the narrator has a definite impact on readers. At times the discrepancy between the embellished narration and the grim subject matter alienates readers. Perhaps this contrast cleverly gives readers a small taste of the picaro's experience. In many of the expressions used by the narrator, he seems to go to great lengths to avoid calling an object or concept by its ordinary name. Thus, an ice cream bar is called "hielo pintado y saborizado" [colored and flavored ice] (p. 241), fruit is referred to as "gérmenes patógenos" [germ pathogenes] (p. 249), a theft is termed "aliviane de fondos" [alleviation of funds] (p. 264), and so forth. For some readers, such expressions could echo the fashion in which bureaucracies create overblown, convoluted terms for common items. Such a reading would likely further alienate readers, appropriate since *El Chanfalla* is presented as a political novel. Other readers could see such expressions as examples of what Victor Shklovsky has termed "defamiliarization."[6] They force us to deal with common, everyday items in an uncommon, unusual way. With either reading, the narrator leads us to a different level of reality.

In summary, the implied author keeps the issue of delving more deeply into reality at the forefront of the text in several major ways. Episodes that illustrate the unfaithfulness of appearances, others that feature fantastic elements, and the narrator's artificial mode of expression all impel readers to deal with varying levels of appearance and reality. Since the book is presented as a political novel, and much of the text's content deals directly with politics in the 1930s, one of the messages that seems to be strongest in the text is the need to probe into the realities of history and politics both past and present. On the surface *El Chanfalla* seems a simple book that shows the adventures of a resilient boy in a harsh city; however, further study reveals a novel that challenges its readers to deal with the complex social, political, and philosophical issues associated with the relationship between appearance and reality.

10

Conclusion

Wherein by way of conclusion it is pointed out that although the narratives examined in this study possess a great many characteristics in common, thus meriting categorization as picaresque, due to differing periods of creation, literary tendencies, and authorial intents, they are as different as Clydesdales and Shetland ponies.

LET US RETURN BRIEFLY TO THE MATTER OF THE PICARESQUE subgenre. In his essay on the picaresque, Claudio Guillén states:

> No work embodies completely the picaresque genre. The genre is not, of course, a novel any more than the equine species is a horse. A genre is a model . . . A genre has stable features, but it also changes, as a precise influence on the work in progress, with the writer, the nation, and the period.[1]

The eight narratives analyzed in chapters two through nine of this study support absolutely Guillén's statement, and in particular the final sentence. The study itself merely makes evident *how* the narratives support Guillén's assertion. Using the picaresque characteristics set forth in the preface and used in the body of this study, the following chart illustrates in a simplified yet concrete way how the picaresque subgenre in Mexico "has stable features, but it also changes."

As this chart readily shows, of the fifteen characteristics we have used as a model for the picaresque subgenre, the eight texts analyzed at length in this study have only six of the elements in common. The six elements (episodic plot, a single protagonist, protean form, alienation, physical survival, and a vast gallery of human types) tell us that these narratives share some very basic structural and thematic ingredients. Structurally, each features an episodic plot wherein episodes are linked by a single character. In the course of the many episodes, the protagonist meets many different character types, thus giving a view of society. Each of the picaros is alienated from his fellow beings, and in an effort merely to stay alive, he, or she in the case of Jesusa Palancares, must resort to practicing a variety of professions. In short, the foregoing sentences describe the essence of picaresque narratives in Mexico.

	1	2	3	4	5a	5b	5c	5d	5e	5f	5g	6	7	8	9
1542 *Naufragios*	X	X	X	X	X	—	X	X	X	—	—	X	X	X	X
1690 *Infortunios*	X	X	X	X	X	—	—	X	X	—	—	X	X	X	X
1816 *El Periquillo*	X	—	X	X	X	—	X	X	X	X	X	X	X	X	X
1832 *Don Catrín*	X	X	X	X	X	X	X	X	X	X	X	X	—	X	X
1938 *La vida inútil*	X	X	X	—	X	X	X	X	X	X	X	—	X	X	X
1941 *El Canillitas*	X	—	—	X	X	X	X	X	X	X	X	—	X	X	X
1969 *Hasta no verte*	X	—	X	X	X	X	X	X	X	X	X	X	X	X	X
1979 *El Chanfalla*	X	X	—	X	X	X	X	X	X	X	X	—	X	X	X

Key to above categories:

1)	Episodic plot	5e)	Alienation
2)	Dizzying rhythm	5f)	Internal instability
3)	Fate rules supreme	5g)	A philosophical bent
4)	Bodily violence	6)	The first-person point of view
5a)	A single protagonist	7)	An unkind, chaotic world
5b	Uncommon origins	8)	Physical survival
5c)	Cunning	9)	A vast gallery of human types
5d)	Protean form		

Analysis of the characteristics *not* shared by the eight narratives proves equally revealing regarding the picaresque in Mexico. When only one narrative lacks an element, we can assume that such an occurrence is peculiar to a text, rather than a pattern in the Mexican picaresque. We see three cases of the foregoing, in that *La vida inútil de Pito Pérez* includes a reduced measure of bodily violence, in that Alonso Ramírez does not show a great deal of cunning, and in that Don Catrín lives in a relatively unthreatening world. Although missing in a single text, the foregoing elements seem to be common to the overwhelming majority of Mexican picaresque narratives.

Six characteristics are absent in more than one text. Let us look at the patterns for each of these characteristics individually. Only five of the narratives feature a rapid-fire pace. The three narratives that do not are heavily steeped in philosophical and *costumbrista* digressions and pauses. Thus, dizzying rhythm is not a strong aspect of the picaresque in Mexico.

In all but two of the narratives the narrator communicates that fate has an overwhelming role in the life of the picaro. Curiously, both of these texts, *El Canillitas* and *El Chanfalla,* are also lacking the first-person point of view. We can conclude that a first-person narrator tends to see himself as helpless much more than a third-person narrator. In other words, picaros perceive themselves as victims, while detached narrators hold picaros responsible for their situations. Furthermore, all three of the texts that utilize the third-person point of view belong to the present century. The influence of realism, with its efforts toward objectivism, seems apparent.

The remaining three characteristics absent in more than one Mexican picaresque narrative have to do with the picaro. *Naufragios* and *Infortunios de Alonso Ramírez* feature protagonists that do not have uncommon origins, internal instability, or a philosophical bent. The absence of internal instability in the picaros of these texts rings logical in that both of the actual texts aimed to depict the protagonist as a stable, constant individual in spite of the monumental challenges he faces. The tendency away from philosophizing also seems logical in these texts because the real-life people, Cabeza de Vaca and Alonso Ramírez, were anxious for their tales of misfortunes and heroism, rather than their ideas, to be distributed. *El Periquillo Sarniento* joins the abovementioned narratives to form the threesome of Mexican picaresque tales that feature picaros lacking uncommon origins. In *Naufragios* and *Infortunios* the narrator/protagonists simply avoid the issue of their origins. The *Periquillo* seems to show that "average" origins for many of the people of the day were less than ideal. Whatever the cause, in all of the Mexican picaresque narratives since 1816, the picaros are depicted as products of uncommon origins.

The chart above further illustrates that *Naufragios* and *Infortunios* conspicuously lack characteristics having to do with the picaro; at the same time both texts feature a full set of the other eight characteristics. These data seem to indicate that these early narratives are fully developed in the sense of technical narrative aspects of the picaresque, while the central hero does not match the picaro model.

Although none of the six narratives since *Infortunios* possesses all fifteen of the picaresque characteristics in the model, the fact that each has a nearly complete set is evidence of the similarities shared by the texts. Thus, even though it appears in a grossly understated form in the chart, we see that without a doubt the picaresque in Mexico "has stable features, but it also changes."

The body of this study illustrates that the chart is truly an understatement in that it does not reflect to what extent certain characteristics are emphasized in certain narratives. For example, although fate is a factor in six of the texts, in none does it play a more prominent role than in *Infortunios de Alonso Ramírez*. The variety of focus used herein to analyze the narratives in the final portion of each chapter constitutes perhaps the greatest evidence that, in spite of their incontestable similarities, the texts differ greatly from one another. By way of illustration, the obvious irony which pervades *Don Catrín de la Fachenda* brought on a study of the quantum distance between its implied author and narrator. A similar study may be productive for the *Periquillo* or even for *Hasta no verte Jesús mío,* but the study would produce different findings from those for *Don Catrín*. By contrast, the same type of analysis would likely reveal very little in *Naufragios* or the three texts with third-person narrators: *La vida inútil de Pito Pérez, El Canillitas,* and *El Chanfalla*.

A brief summary of the outstanding characteristics in each of the works analyzed in detail in this study further accentuates the unique nature of each work. The dizzying rhythm and focus on physical survival highlight *Naufragios*. Using an extreme economy of expression, Cabeza de Vaca makes his adventures come alive for readers. The book's numerous episodes featuring life-threatening situations illustrate perfectly the physical challenges involved in the era of discovery in the New World. Its inclusion in a study on the picaresque is somewhat surprising because it likely predates *Lazarillo de Tormes,* yet it shares obvious kinship with the subgenre.

In *Infortunios de Alonso Ramírez,* as noted above and confirmed in its title, the protagonist seems most thoroughly victimized by fate. To make matters worse for Alonso, each time he works his way to a measure of stability, fate snatches stability away from him, thus creating a dizzying rhythm. Brutal bodily violence, an extremely unkind, unpredictable world, and the theme of physical survival also constitute outstanding picaresque elements in the text. *Infortunios* deserves note also because it seems to be a work of fiction that precedes Fernández de Lizardi.

El Periquillo Sarniento has traditionally been held as the first pure novel from Mexico and Spanish America. To state that it has a philosophical bent strongly understates the case. It is by far the

Mexican picaresque champion in the category of philosophical ramblings. Its author's proposal of societal reform led to a vast, rich array of brilliantly depicted, yet often flawed colonial human types. It also richly depicts outdated, decayed customs in Mexico before independence.

I find the protagonist of *Don Catrín de la Fachenda* one of the most memorable characters in Mexican literature. His pomposity, arrogance, vanity, and disdain for others are matched by his financial and moral bankruptcy. His claim to excellence of blood proves equally groundless. This book also features the entertaining gallery of secondary characters Catrín meets, each of whom has a name symbolic of his personality, as does the protagonist. I believe that of the narratives examined in this study *Don Catrín de la Fachenda* most closely resembles the ideal picaresque model.

The thematically rather than chronologically organized narrative structure of *La vida inútil de Pito Pérez* makes it unique. Thus, one chapter deals with love, or lack thereof, in Pito's life, another deals with his experiences in jails, etc. The protagonist is one of Mexico's most popular fictional figures, who this study proves to be a deceptively complex character. Provincial charm and humor give a distinctive mark to this short piece.

El Canillitas is the first Mexican picaresque text not set in the period contemporary with its writer. Instead, like the *colonialista* literature that had been in fashion some years earlier in Mexican prose, this narrative takes place in colonial times. Rather than focus on the protagonist, as happens in *Don Catrín* and *La vida inútil,* or on the protagonist's actions, as in *Naufragios* and *Infortunios,* this text is similar to the *Periquillo* in that it seeks to present the customs and environment of a time period in Mexico. As opposed to the *Periquillo* and the traditional picaresque novel, however, its look at society proves nostalgic rather than critical. The style feigns antiquated speech and a pleasant dose of humor laces its pages, as chapter seven studies. Like the *Periquillo,* because of its length only dedicated readers conquer the entire text.

Hasta no verte Jesús mío excels in its presentation of a rounded protagonist. Of the picaros studied herein, Jesusa Palancares seems the most human. Not only do we see the events, joys, and hardships of her life, but we hear her manner of speech, her concerns, and her opinions. This text comes across as an oral autobiography, while many of the other texts seem self-conscious. This text is also outstanding in that it reveals the impact of the revolution and other major events in twentieth-century Mexico on an individual.

El Chanfalla, like *El Canillitas,* takes place in a setting different from the time of writing. The action occurs primarily in Mexico City in the 1930s, and as in *El Canillitas,* we get the impression that the author is vitally concerned with depicting an era, while the picaro and his story hold secondary importance. Its structure is unique to this set of narratives in that during the first half of the book, episodes from the picaro's early life are intercalated with episodes from the main story line. The cast of secondary characters Chanfalla meets is an especially varied and unusual group, with a heavy emphasis on the lower classes. *El Chanfalla* also stands out due to the presence of fantastic elements in the text, such as talking animals and miraculously self-propagating ice cream bars. In addition, of our set of picaros, Chanfalla is the youngest, most naive, and least prepared to deal with the world around him.

In conclusion, that authors have employed picaresque conventions from time to time throughout the history of Mexico attests to the usefulness and resilience of the subgenre, regardless of literary, political, and economic variables. Even though these works have many characteristics in common, each is a unique creation. To extend Claudio Guillén's analogy cited at the beginning of this chapter, the relationship between these texts is akin to that of Shetland ponies, Clydesdales, and Quarter horses—they all form part of the equine species, but each features unique, delightful traits. Regardless of era, style, intent, or technique, the texts which populate the picaresque family in Mexico are delightful, probing, unique works of art. Without a doubt, authors in Mexico and throughout the world will continue to tap the conventions of the picaresque to make statements about society, to delve into the inner workings of human beings, and to delight readers with good humor.

Notes

Preface

1. Claudio Guillén, "Toward a Definition of the Picaresque," in *Literature as System: Essays Toward the Theory of Literary History* (Princeton: Princeton University Press, 1971), 71–106.
2. Stuart Miller, *The Picaresque Novel* (Cleveland: The Press of Case Western Reserve University, 1967).
3. Ulrich Wicks, "The Nature of Picaresque Narrative: A Modal Approach," *PMLA* 89 (1974): 240–49.
4. Miller, 9–20; Guillén, 84–85.
5. Miller, 21–27.
6. Miller, 28–35; Wicks, 243–44.
7. Miller, 36–39; Wicks, 247.
8. Guillén, 94.
9. Wicks, 246.
10. Miller, 47–55.
11. Wicks, 245.
12. Guillén, 76.
13. Miller, 70–77; Wicks, 247; Guillén, 92.
14. Guillén, 80.
15. Miller, 78.
16. Ibid., 86–94.
17. Guillén, 76, 81–82.
18. Guillén, 81–82; Miller, 98–100; Wicks, 244–45.
19. Miller, 56–69.
20. Guillén, 83.
21. Wicks, 246.
22. Guillén, 83–84; Wicks, 245.

Chapter 1: A Survey of Partially Picaresque Narratives

1. Two studies have tackled the picaresque in the entirety of Latin America. The most complete is María Casas de Faunce, *La novela picaresca latinoamericana* [The Latin American Picaresque Novel] (Madrid: Cupsa, 1977), which tries to examine and point out picaresque elements in all pertinent Latin American novels. Luis Leal, "Picaresca hispanoamericana: de Oquendo a Lizardi" [Spanish-American Picaresque: From Oquendo to Lizardi], *Estudios de literatura hispanoamericana en honor a José J. Arrom* [Studies on Spanish-American Literature in Honor of José J. Arrom] (Chapel Hill: University of North Carolina

Press, 1974), 47–58, is less ambitious. It looks at the existence of picaros in Latin America before the appearance in 1816 of Lizardi's *El Periquillo Sarniento.*

Likewise, two studies have broadly approached the picaresque in Mexico. Carol Roark Blackburn, "The Picaresque Novel of Mexico" (Ph.D. diss., University of Illinois, 1969), is an unpublished, and now outdated, yet rather complete study of picaresque aspects of Mexican novels. Luis Leal, "Pícaros y léperos en la narrativa mexicana" [Picaros and *Léperos* in Mexican Narrative], *La picaresca: orígenes, textos y estructuras* [The Picaresque: Origins, Texts, and Structures] (Madrid: Fundación Universitaria Española, 1979), 1033–40, focuses on Mexican picaro types.

2. Alvar Núñez Cabeza de Vaca, *Naufragios* (Madrid: Espasa-Calpe, 1922). An extensive study of this book is found in chapter 2.

3. Hernán Cortés, "Carta segunda," in *Cartas de relación de la conquista de México* (Madrid: Espasa-Calpe, 1945), 33–100.

4. Bernal Díaz de Castillo, *Historia verdadera de la conquista de la Nueva España* (Madrid: Espasa-Calpe, 1955).

5. Carlos de Sigüenza y Góngora, *Infortunios de Alonso Ramírez* (San Juan de Puerto Rico: Editorial Cordillera, 1967); José Joaquín Fernández de Lizardi, *El Periquillo Sarniento* (Mexico City: Porrúa, 1949). Extensive studies of these books are found in chapters 3 and 4.

6. José Joaquín Fernández de Lizardi, *Don Catrín de la Fachenda* (Mexico City: Cultura, 1944); and *La educación de las mujeres o la Quijotita y su prima* (Mexico City: Cámara Méxicana del Libro, 1942). An extensive study of *Don Catrín* is found in chapter 5.

7. Ignacio Rodríguez Galván, *Tras un mal nos vienen ciento,* in *Novelas cortas de varios autores,* vol. 1 (Mexico City: Imp de V. Agüero, 1901), 213–62.

8. Manuel Paynó, *El fistol del diablo* (Mexico City: Porrúa, 1967); Luis G. Inclán, *Astucia, el jefe del los hermanos de la hoja, o los charros contrabandistas de la rama* (Mexico City: Porrúa, 1966).

9. Vicente Riva Palacio, *Monja y casada, virgen y mártir: Historia de los tiempos de la inquisición* (Mexico City: Ediciones León Sánchez, n.d.); *Martín Garatuza* (Mexico City: Ediciones León Sánchez, n.d.).

10. José T. de Cuéllar, *Historia de Chucho el Ninfo,* Colección de escritores mexicanos, vol. 45 (Mexico City: Porrúa, 1947).

11. Manuel Balbontín, *Memorias de un muerto* (Mexico City: Imp. de I. Cumplido, 1888).

12. Emilio Rabasa, *La Bola* and *La gran ciencia* (Mexico City: Porrúa, 1948); *El cuarto poder* and *Moneda falsa* (Mexico City: Porrúa, 1948).

13. Porfirio Parra, *Pacotillas* (Mexico City: Premia editora, 1982).

14. Manuel H. San Juan, *El señor gobernador* (Mexico City: Imprenta y Encuadernación de M. Nava, 1901).

15. José Rubén Romero, *La vida inútil de Pito Pérez* (Mexico City: Porrúa, 1981). An extensive study of this novel is found in chapter 6.

16. Juan Rulfo, *Pedro Páramo,* 2nd ed. (Mexico City: Fondo de Cultura Económica, 1981); Carlos Fuentes, *La muerte de Artemio Cruz* (Mexico City: Bruguera, 1981).

17. Artemio de Valle-Arizpe, *El Canillitas: Novela de burlas y donaires,* 4th ed. (Mexico City: Edición y Distribución Ibero Americana de Publicaciones, 1947). An extensive study of this novel is found in chapter 7.

18. Jesús R. Guerrero, *Los olvidados* (Mexico City: Estampa, 1944).

19. Carol Roark Blackburn, "The Picaresque Novel of Mexico" (Ph.D. diss., University of Illinois, 1969).

20. Leopoldo Zamora Plowes, *Quince uñas y Casanova, aventureros: Novela histórica picaresca* (Mexico City: Talleres Gráficos de *La nación*, 1945).

21. María Casas de Faunce, *La novela picaresca latinoamericana* (Madrid: Cupsa, 1977), 141.

22. Enrique García Campos, *Garambullo: Historia de un pícaro sin fortuna* (Mexico City, 1945).

23. Blackburn, 127.

24. Rogelio Barriga Rivas, *Río humano* (Mexico City: Ediciones Botas, 1949).

25. Ermilo Abreu Gómez, *Tata Lobo* (Mexico City: Fondo de Cultura Económica, 1952).

26. Casas de Faunce, 196.

27. José Valdovinos Garza, *El hombre que fue dos* (Mexico City: Catalina, 1963).

28. José Agustín, *La tumba: revelaciones de un adolescente* (Mexico City: Organización Editorial Novaro, 1966); Gustavo Sainz, *Gazapo* (Mexico City: Joaquín Mortiz, 1965). The "Onda" refers to a literary tendency of the early 1960's in Mexico characterized by narratives featuring the alienated, upper-class youth of Mexico City, their slang (from which comes the term "onda"), and their sex, drugs, and rock-and-roll existence.

29. Elena Poniatowska, *Hasta no verte Jesús mío* (Mexico City: Era, 1969). An extensive study of this novel is found in chapter 8.

30. Armando Ramírez, *Chin-Chin el teporocho* (Mexico City: Organización Editorial Novaro, 1972).

31. Ibid., 82.

32. Gustavo Sainz, *La princesa del palacio de hierro* (Mexico City: Joaquín Mortiz, 1974).

33. Gonzalo Martré, *El Chanfalla* (Mexico City: Editorial V Siglos, 1979); Luis Zapata, *Las aventuras, desventuras y sueños de Adonís García, El vampiro de la colonia Roma* (Mexico City: Grijalbo, 1979). An extensive study of *El Chanfalla* is found in chapter 9.

34. Carlos Eduardo Turón, *Sobre esta piedra* (Mexico City: Oasis, 1981).

35. Angeles Mastretta, *Arráncame la vida* (Mexico City: Océano, 1985).

36. José Madrigal Mora, *El general Hilachas* (Mexico City: Fondo de Cultura Económica, 1985).

CHAPTER 2: *NAUFRAGIOS*

1. See, for example, Fernando Alegría, *Breve historia de la novela hispanoamericana* [Brief History of the Spanish-American Novel] (Mexico City: Ediciones de Andrea, 1959), 7–13; Antonio Curcio Altamar, "La ausencia de novela en el Nuevo Reino" [The Absence of Novels in the New Kingdom], in *La novela hispanoamericana,* ed. Juan Loveluck, 3rd ed. (Chile: Editorial Universitaria, 1969): 51–59.

2. Gabriel García Márquez, "The Solitude of Latin America," *New York Times,* 6 February 1983, sec. IV, p. 17.

3. Ibid.

4. Alvar Núñez Cabeza de Vaca, *Naufragios* (Madrid: Espasa-Calpe, 1922). All references to *Naufragios* by page number in chapter 2 come from this edition.

5. Cyclone Covey, introduction to *Adventures in the Unknown Interior of America* (New York: Collier Books, 1961), 7.

6. Complete translations of *Naufragios:* Cyclone Covey, trans., *Adventures in the Unknown Interior of America* (New York: Collier Books, 1961); Fanny Bandelier, trans., *The Journey of Alvar Núñez Cabeza de Vaca and his Companions from Florida to the Pacific, 1528–1536* (New York: Allerton Book Co., 1922); Buckingham Smith, trans., *Shipwrecks of Alvar Núñez Cabeza de Vaca* (Washington, D.C.: Published for private distribution by George W. Riggs Jr., 1851).

The partial translation was performed by Haniel Long in *The Power Within Us: Cabeza de Vaca's Relation of His Journey from Florida to the Pacific 1528–1536* (New York: Duell, Sloan and Pearce, 1944).

The paraphrased versions of *Naufragios:* Samuel Purchas, *His Pilgrimes* (London: 1613), and Cleve Hallenbeck, *Alvar Núñez Cabeza de Vaca: the Journey and Route of the First European to Cross the Continent of North America, 1534–1536* (Glendale, Calif.: The Arthur H. Clark Company, 1940).

A brief summary of some of the major editions of *Naufragios* and its translations is found on pages 51–53 of Trinidad Barrera, "Introducción," *Naufragios* (Madrid: Alianza Editorial, 1985), 7–55.

7. Biographies of Cabeza de Vaca: Andrés Bellogín García, *Vida y hazañas de Alvar Núñez Cabeza de Vaca* (Madrid: Editorial Voluntad, 1982); José B. Fernández, *Alvar Núñez Cabeza de Vaca: The Forgotten Chronicler* (Miami: Ediciones Universal, 1975); Carlos Lacalle, *Noticia sobre Alvar Núñez Cabeza de Vaca: Hazañas americanas de un caballero andaluz* (Madrid: Instituto de Cultura Hispánica, 1961); John Upton Terrell, *Journey into Darkness: Cabeza de Vaca's Expedition Across North America, 1528–1536* (London: Jarrolds, 1964); Antonio Urdapilleta, *Andanzas y desventuras de Alvar Núñez Cabeza de Vaca* (Madrid: Gráficas Valera, 1949).

Studies on Cabeza de Vaca's route: James Newton Baskett, "A Study of the Route of Cabeza de Vaca," *The Texas Historical Quarterly* 10, no. 1 (1907): 246–79; 10, no. 2 (1907): 308–40; Bethel Coopwood, "Route of Cabeza de Vaca in Texas," *The Texas Historical Quarterly* 3, no. 4 (1899): 108–40; O. W. Williams, "The Route of Cabeza de Vaca in Texas," *The Texas Historical Association Quarterly* 3, no. 3 (1899): 54–64.

Historical novels based on Cabeza de Vaca: Morris Bishop, *The Odyssey of Cabeza de Vaca* (New York: The Century Co., 1933); Camilla Campbell, *Galleons Sail Westward* (Dallas: Mathis, Van Nort and Col, 1939); Oakley Hall, *The Children of the Sun* (New York: Atheneum, 1983); Daniel Panger, *Black Ulysses* (Athens, Ohio: Ohio University Press, 1982); Frank G. Slaughter, *Apalachee Gold: The Fabulous Adventures of Cabeza de Vaca* (Garden City, N.Y.: Doubleday, 1954); Maia Wojciechowska, *Odyssey of Courage: The Story of Alvar Núñez Cabeza de Vaca* (New York: Atheneum, 1965).

Epic poem containing a canto based on Cabeza de Vaca: Walter Brooks Drayton Henderson, *The new Argonautica, an heroic poem in eight cantos, of the voyage among the stars of the immortal spirits of Sir Walter Raleigh, Sir Francis Drake, Ponce de Leon and Nuñez da Vaca . . .* (New York: The Macmillan Co., 1928).

Paintings: Ted Ettore De Grazia, *De Grazia Paints Cabeza de Vaca: The First Non-Indian in Texas, New Mexico, and Arizona 1527–1536* (Tucson: University of Arizona Press, 1973).

8. Hernando Téllez, "La novela en Latinoamérica," in *La novela hispanoamericana,* ed. Juan Loveluck, 3rd ed. (Chile: Editorial Universitaria, 1969), on

pp. 44–45, calls the work novelesque. See also John E. Englekirk, et al., *An Outline History of Spanish American Literature* 3rd ed. (New York: Appleton-Century-Crofts, 1965), 14.

9. David Lagmanovich, "Los *Naufragios* de Alvar Núñez como construcción narrativa," *Kentucky Romance Quarterly* 25 (1978): 27–37.

10. Robert E. Lewis, "Los *Naufragios* de Alvar Núñez: historia y ficción," *Revista Iberoamericana* 48 (1982): 681–94. The "Prohemio," written to Carlos V, appeared in the first two editions of the text (1542 and 1555). Very few editions of the text since that time have included it.

11. Vito Galeota, "Appunti per un'analisi letteraria de *Naufragios* de Alvar Núñez Cabeza de Vaca, *Annali Instituto Universitario Orientales Napoli-Sezione Romanza* 25 (1983): 471–97.

12. Lee W. Dowling, "Story vs. Discourse in the Chronicle of the Indies: Alvar Núñez Cabeza de Vaca's *Relación*," *Hispanic Journal* 5, no. 2 (1984): 89–99.

13. Pedro Lastra, "Espacios de Alvar Núñez: Las transformaciones de una escritura," *Revista chilena de literatura* 23 (1984): 93–94.

14. Lagmanovich, p. 29.

15. Sandra Rosenberg, "Travel Literature and the Picaresque Novel," *Enlightenment Essays* 2 (1971): 40. A similar statement appears in Percy G. Adams, *Travel Literature and the Evolution of the Novel* (Lexington: The University Press of Kentucky, 1983), 198–99: "Of all satiric fiction the kind perhaps most closely and most often associated with travel literature is that vaguely and uncertainly called 'picaresque.'"

16. See, for example, Frank W. Chandler, *Romances of Roguery: An Episode in the History of the Novel, The Picaresque Novel in Spain* (New York: Columbia University Press, 1899): 184–87; and Christine J. Whitbourn, "Moral Ambiguity in the Spanish Picaresque Tradition," in *Knaves and Swindlers: Essays on the Picaresque Novel in Europe* (London: Oxford University Press, 1974), 1–5.

17. Jesús Helí Hernández, *Antecedentes Italianos de la Novela Picaresca Española: Aspectos Literarios y Lingüísticos* (Madrid: Ediciones José Porrúa Turanzas, 1982). The bulk of this book deals with possible ties the picaresque tradition has with Italian literature. The introductory chapter provides a summary of what other critics have written regarding the picaresque's relationship to other non-Spanish literatures.

CHAPTER 3: *INFORTUNIOS DE ALONSO RAMÍREZ*

1. Carlos de Sigüenza y Góngora, *Infortunios de Alonso Ramírez* (San Juan de Puerto Rico: Editorial Cordillera, 1967). All page number references to *Infortunios* in this study come from this edition.

2. Bo Schembechler and Mitch Albom, *Bo* (New York: Warner Books, 1989).

3. Bob Greene, "Bo Schembechler could take a page from Woody's book," *Detroit Free Press,* 31 October 1989, sec. B, p. 11.

4. Elena Poniatowska, *Hasta no verte Jesús mío* (Mexico City: Era, 1969). Chapter 8 focuses on Poniatowska's "novel."

5. The following statements represent a sampling from literary histories and anthologies: Carlos González Peña, *Historia de la literatura mexicana: Desde los orígenes hasta nuestros días* [History of Mexican Literature: From Origins Through Our Times], 9th ed. (Mexico City: Porrúa, 1966), 99, calls *Infortunios* "nuestra primera novela" [our first novel] (99); Fernando Alegría, *Breve historia de la novela hispanoamericana* [Brief History of the Spanish American Novel]

(Mexico City: Ediciones de Andrea, 1959), 16, includes it in a long list of works written prior to the *Periquillo,* admitting that critics see in them novelistic characteristics, but stating emphatically that "Ninguna de las obras citadas es novela y toda discusión al respecto es enteramente ociosa" [None of the works cited is a novel and all discussion on the topic is entirely idle]; Angel Flores, *The Literature of Spanish America,* vol. 1 (New York: Las Américas, 1966), 212–13, states that "In *Infortunios de Alonso Ramírez* Sigüenza y Góngora gave Latin America its first novel"; John Brushwood, *Mexico in Its Novel: A Nation's Search for Identity* (Austin: University of Texas Press, 1966), 62, says of the referent that "A novelist might indeed have made a real novel of it"; Heriberto García Rivas, *Historia de la literatura mexicana* [History of Mexican Literature] vol. 1 (Mexico City: Textos Universitarios, 1971), 355, classifies the text as a "libro de viajes" [travel book]; Galo René Pérez, *Historia crítitca de la novela hispanoamericana* [Critical History of the Spanish-American Novel] (Bogotá: Círculo de Lectores, 1977), 17, insists that the *Periquillo* is Spanish America's first novel and mentions *Infortunios* in a long list of works he calls "antecedentes del género" [antecedents of the genre]. Willebaldo Bazarte Cerdán, "La Primera Novela Mexicana" [The First Mexican Novel], *Humanismo* 50–51, no. 7 (1958): 106, has it both ways: "*Infortunios de Alonso Ramírez* es nuestra primera novela, y . . . *El Periquillo Sarniento* es nuestra primera novela por cuanto a su técnica, estilo, desarrollo, envergadura, tema, tratado, etc" [*Infortunios de Alonso Ramírez* is our first novel, and . . . *El Periquillo Sarniento* is our first novel with regard to its technique, style, development, importance, theme, treatment, etc.].

6. See the studies by Alba Vallés Formosa, Raúl Castagnino, David Lagmanovich, María Casas de Faunce, Julie Greer Johnson, Raquel Chang-Rodríguez, and Aníbal González. Lucrecio Pérez Blanco posits an alternate theory to tying *Infortunios* to the picaresque. He surmises that it is modeled after the tradition of Greek novels. See also the articles by Alan Soons and James Cummins, which deal with matters other than generic classification and the picaresque tradition.

7. David Lagmanovich, "Para una caracterización de *Infortunios de Alonso Ramírez*" [Toward a Characterization of *Infortunios de Alonso Ramírez*], *Sin Nombre* 2, no. 5 (1974): 9.

8. The term "tremendismo" is often associated with Camilo José Cela's *La familia de Pascual Duarte,* with its emphasis on the harshness and bitterness of life, and raw, detatched descriptions of human suffering.

Chapter 4: *El Periquillo Sarniento*

1. José Joaquín Fernández de Lizardi, *El Periquillo Sarniento* (Mexico City: Porrúa, 1959). All references by page number to the *Periquillo* in this chapter come from this edition of the text.

2. Jefferson Rea Spell, *Bridging the Gap* (Mexico City: Libros de Mexico City), 143–48, and María Casas de Faunce, *La novela picaresca latinoamericana* (Madrid: Cupsa, 1977), 32–34, expound on the literary and historical context of the *Periquillo.*

3. David William Foster, *Mexican Literature: A Bibliography of Secondary Sources* (Metuchen, N.J.: The Scarecrow Press, 1981), 126–34, contains bibliographical information on the text's criticism.

4. Spell, p. 8.

5. Ibid, p. 271.

6. Nancy Vogeley, "Defining the 'Colonial Reader': *El Periquillo Sarniento*," *PMLA* 102 (1987): 784–800.

CHAPTER 5: *DON CATRÍN DE LA FACHENDA*

1. José Joaquín Fernández de Lizardi, *Don Catrín de la Fachenda* (Mexico City: Porrúa, 1959). Unless otherwise indicated, all references by page number to *Don Catrín* in this chapter come from this edition of the text.

2. Angel Flores, *Historia y Antología del Cuento y la Novela en Hispanoamérica* (New York: Las Américas Publishing Co., 1959), 11–12.

3. John E. Englekirk, et al, *An Outline History of Spanish American Literature,* 3rd ed. (New York: Appleton-Century Crofts, 1965), 48.

4. Enrique Anderson Imbert, *Spanish-American Literature: A History,* trans. John V. Falconieri (Detroit: Wayne State University, 1963), 204–5.

5. Fernando Alegría, *Breve historia de la novela hispanoamericana* (Mexico City: Ediciones de Andrea, 1959), 25–26.

6. John S. Brushwood, *Mexico in Its Novel: A Nation's Search for Identity* (Austin: University of Texas Press, 1966), 67.

7. Jefferson Rea Spell, *Bridging The Gap* (Mexico City: Libros de México, 1971), 231. *Bridging The Gap* contains Spell's *The Life and Works of José Joaquín Fernández de Lizardi,* which was originally published in 1931 in Philadelphia at the University of Pennsylvania.

8. Jefferson Rea Spell, "Prólogo" [Prologue], *Don Catrín de la Fachenda y Noches tristes y día alegre* (Mexico City: Porrúa, 1959), x.

9. Robert L. Bancroft, "The *Periquillo Sarniento* and *Don Catrín de la Fachenda:* Which is the Masterpiece?", *Revista Hispánica Moderna* 34 (1968): 533–38, and John Pawlowski, "*Periquillo* and *Catrín:* Comparison and Contrast," *Hispania* 58 (1975): 830–842.

10. Paul W. Borgeson, Jr., "Problemas de técnica narrativa en dos *novellas* de Lizardi" [Problems of Narrative Tecnique, in two *novellas* of Lizardi], *Hispania* 69 (1986): 504–11.

11. María Casas de Faunce, *La novela picaresca latinoamericana* (Madrid: Cupsa, 1977).

12. Jefferson Rea Spell, *Bridging The Gap* (Mexico City: Libros de México, 1971), 231.

13. Charles C. Cumberland, *Mexico: The Struggle for Modernity* (London: Oxford University Press, 1968), 113–40.

14. Spell, 107–20.

15. The footnote referred to here is inexplicably absent for the 1959 Porrúa edition of the text. In the Caillet-Bois edition it appears on page 106. In the 1944 Cultura edition it appears on page 81. Equally as puzzling, the Caillet-Bois edition refers the reader to a different section of the text than does the Cultura edition.

CHAPTER 6: *LA VIDA INÚTIL DE PITO PÉREZ*

1. José Rubén Romero, *La vida inútil de Pito Pérez* (Mexico City: Porrúa, 1981). All references by page number to the Spanish version of *La vida inútil* in this chapter come from this edition of the text. Likewise, all references by page number to the English translation of the novel come from *The Futile Life of Pito Perez,* trans. William O. Cord (Englewood Cliffs, N.J.: Prentice-Hall, 1966).

2. Bradley Smith, *Mexico: A History in Art* (New York: Doubleday, 1968), 286.

3. On the novel's relationship to the picaresque see Gastón Lafarga, *La evolución literaria de Rubén Romero* [The Literary Evolution of Rubén Romero] (Paris: Gouyardín, 1939), Ernest Richard Moore, *Novelistas de la revolución mexicana: José Rubén Romero* [Novelists of the Mexican Revolution: José Rubén Romero] (La Habana: La Verónica, 1940), Raúl Arreola Cortés, "José Rubén Romero; vida y obra" [José Rubén Romero: Life and Work], *Revista Hispánica Moderna* 12 (1946): 7–34, and Manuel Pedro González, *Trayectoria de la novela en México* [Trajectory of the Novel in Mexico] (Mexico City: Botas, 1951), 243–44.

Ulrich Wicks, "Onlyman," *Mosaic* 8, No. 3 (1975): 21–47, discusses the novel's narrative technique.

4. On the novel's use of language, see Gastón Lafarga (cited in note 3) and Gilberto González y Contreras, *El hombre que supo ver* [The Man Who Learned to See] (La Habana: La Verónica, 1940).

On the novel's humor, see R. Anthony Castagnaro, "Rubén Romero and the Novel of the Mexican Revolution," *Hispania* 36 (1953): 300–304, and Arturo Torres-Ríoseco, "Humor in Hispanic Literature," *Aspects of Spanish-American Literature* (Seattle: University of Washington Press, 1963), 3–30.

5. See Wicks (cited in note 3) and Tamara Holzapfel, "Soledad y rebelión en *La vida inútil de Pito Pérez*" [Loneliness and Rebellion in *La vida inútil de Pito Pérez*] *Revista iberoamericana* 89 (1974): 681–87.

6. Ewart E. Phillips, "The Genesis of Pito Pérez," *Hispania* 47 (1964): 698–702.

7. Ned J. Davison, "La composición de *La vida inútil de Pito Pérez*" [The Composition of *La Vida inútil de Pito Pérez*] *Sobre Eduardo Barrios y otros: estudios y crónicas* [On Eduardo Barrios and Others: Studies and Chronicles] (Albuquerque: Foreign Books, 1966), 13–17.

8. Phillips, 698.

9. Manuel Pedro González, *Trayectoria de la novela en México* (Mexico City: Botas, 1951), 226.

10. Although the idea originates with Barthes, the format used in this study follows the one used in a study by John S. Brushwood, "Codes of Character Definition: Jorge Isaac's *María*," *Genteel Barbarism: New Readings of Nineteenth-Century Spanish-American Novels* (Lincoln: University of Nebraska Press, 1981), 82–106.

11. Rolande Barthes, *S/Z: An Essay* (New York: Hill and Wang, 1974), 5–6.

12. An example is given in Brushwood, 86.

13. John S. Brushwood, *Mexico in Its Novel* (Austin: University of Texas Press, 1966), 223.

CHAPTER 7: *EL CANILLITAS*

1. Artemio de Valle-Arizpe, *El Canillitas: Novela de burlas y donaires,* 4th ed. (Mexico City: Edición y Distribución Ibero Americana de Publicaciones, 1947). Unless otherwise indicated, all references by page number to *El Canillitas* in this chapter come from this edition of the text.

2. John S. Brushwood, *Mexico in Its Novel* (Austin: University of Texas Press, 1966), 187.

3. Ermilo Abreu Gómez, review of *El Canillitas,* by Artemio de Valle-Arizpe, *Letras de México,* 15 July 1941, 5.

4. Manuel Pedro González, *Trayectoria de la novela en México* (Mexico City: Botas, 1951), 231.

5. Roberto Maximiano Acevedo, "Vida y obra de Artemio de Valle-Arizpe" [Life and Work of Artemio de Valle-Arizpe] (Ph.D. diss. University of Arizona, 1972), v.

CHAPTER 8: *HASTA NO VERTE JESÚS MÍO*

1. Elena Poniatowska, *Hasta no verte Jesús mío* (Mexico City: Era, 1969). Unless otherwise indicated, all references by page number to *Hasta no verte* in this chapter come from this edition of the text.
2. "El premio nacional del periodismo por primera vez concedido a una mujer" [National Prize for Journalism Given to a Woman for the First Time], *Fem* 2, No. 6 (1978): 29.
3. Elena Poniatowska, *Querido Diego, te abraza Quiela* (Mexico City: Era, 1978); Elena Poniatowska, *La noche de Tlatelolco* (Mexico City: Era, 1971).
4. John S. Brushwood, *La novela mexicana (1967–1982)* (Mexico City: Grijalbo, 1984), 17–20.
5. Elena Poniatowska, "Hasta no verte, Jesús mío," *Vuelta* 24 (November 1978): 10.
6. Joel Hancock, "Elena Poniatowska"s *Hasta no verte Jesús mío:* the Remaking of the Image of Woman," *Hispania* 66 (1983): 353.
7. Monique J. Lemaitre, "Jesusa Palancares y la dialéctica de la emancipación femenina" [Jesusa Palancares and the Dialectic of Feminine Emancipation] *Revista Iberoamericana* 51 (1985): 751–63.
8. Edward H. Friedman, "The Marginated Narrator: *Hasta no verte Jesús mío* and the Eloquence of Repression," *The Antiheroine's Voice: Narrative Discourse and the Transformation of the Picaresquè* (Columbia: University of Missouri Press, 1987), 170–187.
9. Although the terms and ideas come from Gérard Genette, *Narrative Discourse: An Essay in Method,* trans. Jane E. Lewin (Ithaca, N.Y.: Cornell University Press, 1980), 86–112, this passage comes from a succinct summary in John S. Brushwood, *Genteel Barbarism* (Lincoln: University of Nebraska Press, 1981), 26.
10. Gérard Genette, 113–60. Genette refers to this phenomenon in this chapter on "Frequency." He uses the term "iterative narrative" to describe "narrating one time what happened n times" (p. 116).

CHAPTER 9: *EL CHANFALLA*

1. Gonzalo Martré, *El Chanfalla* (Mexico City: Editorial V Siglos, 1979). Unless otherwise indicated, all references by page number to *El Chanfalla* in this chapter come from this edition of the text.
2. John S. Brushwood, *La novela mexicana (1967–1982)* (Mexico City: Grijalbo, 1984), 17–20.
3. Ignacio Trejo Fuentes, review of *El Chanfalla,* "¿Es *El Chanfalla* una novela picaresca?" [Is *El Chanfalla* a Picaresque Novel?] *Plural* 96 (September 1979): 62–65.
4. Wolfgang A. Luchting, review of *El Chanfalla, World Literature Today* 54 (1980): 258.
5. John S. Brushwood, *La novela mexicana (1967–1982)* (Mexico City: Grijalbo, 1984), 100.
6. Victor Shkolvsky, "Art as Technique," *Russian Formalist Criticism,* trans.

Lee T. Lemon and Marion J. Reis (Lincoln: University of Nebraska Press, 1965), 12–13.

Chapter 10: Conclusion

1. Claudio Guillén, *Literature as System: Essays Toward the Theory of Literary History* (Princeton: Princeton University Press, 1971), 72–73.

Bibliography

Principal Narratives Cited

Fernández de Lizardi, José Joaquín. *Don Catrín de la Fachenda y fragmentos de otras obras.* Edited by Jefferson Rea Spell. Mexico City: Cultura, 1944.

———. *Don Catrín de la Fachenda.* Edited by Julio Caillet-Bois. Buenos Aires: Universitaria de Buenos Aires, 1967.

———. *Don Catrín de la Fachenda y Noches tristes y día alegre.* Edited by Jefferson Rea Spell. Mexico City: Porrúa, 1959.

———. *El Periquillo Sarniento.* Mexico City: Porrúa, 1949.

Martré, Gonzalo. *El Chanfalla.* Mexico City: Editorial V Siglos, 1979.

Núñez Cabeza de Vaca, Alvar. *Naufragios.* Madrid: Espasa-Calpe, 1922.

Poniatowska, Elena. *Hasta no verte Jesús mío.* Mexico City: Era, 1969.

Rubén Romero, José. *La vida inútil de Pito Pérez.* 28th ed. Mexico City: Porrúa, 1981.

Sigüenza y Góngora, Carlos de. *Infortunios de Alonso Ramírez.* San Juan, Puerto Rico: Editorial Cordillera, 1967.

Valle-Arizpe, Artemio de. *El Canillitas: Novela de burlas y donaires.* 4th ed. Mexico City: Edición y Distribución Ibero Americana de Publicaciones, 1947.

Other Narratives Cited

Abreu Gómez, Ermilo. *Tata Lobo.* Mexico City: Fondo de Cultura Económica, 1952.

Agustín, José. *La tumba: Revelaciones de un adolescente.* Mexico City: Organización Editorial Novaro, 1966.

Azuela, Mariano. *La luciérnaga.* In *3 novelas de Mariano Azuela.* Colección popular, no. 89. Mexico City: Fondo de Cultura Económica, 1958.

Balbontín, Manuel. *Memorias de un muerto.* Mexico City: Imp. de I. Cumplido, 1888.

Barriga Rivas, Rogelio. *Río humano.* Mexico City: Ediciones Botas, 1949.

Cortés, Hernán. "Carta segunda." In *Cartas de relación de la conquista de México,* 33–110. Madrid: Espasa-Calpe, 1945.

Cuéllar, José T. de. *Historia de Chucho el Ninfo.* Colección de escritores mexicanos, vol. 45. Mexico City: Porrúa, 1947.

Díaz del Castillo, Bernal. *Historia verdadera de la conquista de la Nueva España.* Madrid: Espasa-Calpe, 1955.

Fernández de Lizardi, José Joaquín. *La educación de las mujeres o la Quijotita y su prima.* Mexico City: Cámara Mexicana del Libro, 1942.

Fuentes, Carlos. *La muerte de Artemio Cruz*. Mexico City: Bruguera, 1981.

García Campos, Enrique. *Garambullo: Historia de un pícaro sin fortuna*. Mexico City: 1945.

Guerrero, Jesús R. *Los olvidados*. Mexico City: Estampa, 1944.

Inclán, Luis G. *Astucia, el jefe de los hermanos de la hoja, o los charros contrabandistas de la rama*. Mexico City: Porrúa, 1966.

López y Fuentes, Gregorio. *Campamento*. 1931.

———. *El indio*. New York: W. W. Norton & Co., 1940.

———. *Tierra: La revolución agraria en México*. 2nd ed. Mexico City: Ediciones Botas, 1946.

Madrigal Mora, José. *El general Hilachas*. Mexico City: Fondo de Cultura Económica, 1985.

Magdaleno, Mauricio. *Resplandor*. 2nd ed. Buenos Aires: Espasa-Calpe, 1950.

Mastretta, Angeles. *Arráncame la vida*. Mexico City: Océano, 1985.

Parra, Porfirio. *Pacotillas*. Mexico City: Premia editora, 1982.

Paynó, Manuel. *El fistol del diablo*. Mexico City: Porrúa, 1967.

Poniatowska, Elena. *La noche de Tlatelolco*. Mexico City: Era, 1971.

———. *Querido Diego, te abraza Quiela*. Mexico City: Era, 1978.

Rabasa, Emilio. *La Bola* y *La gran ciencia*. Mexico City: Porrúa, 1948.

———. *El cuarto poder* y *Moneda falsa*. Mexico City: Porrúa, 1948.

Ramírez, Armando. *Chin-Chin el teporocho*. Mexico City: Organización Editorial Novaro, 1972.

Riva Palacio, Vicente. *Monja y casada, virgen y mártir: Historia de los tiempos de la inquisición*. Mexico City: Ediciones León Sánchez, n.d.

———. *Martín Garatuza*. Mexico City: Ediciones León Sánchez, n.d.

Rodríguez Galván, Ignacio. *Tras un mal nos vienen ciento*. In vol. 1 of *Novelas cortas de varios autores*, 213–62. Mexico City: Imp de V. Agüero, 1901.

Rulfo, Juan. *Pedro Páramo*. 2nd ed. Mexico City: Fondo de Cultura Económica, 1981.

Sainz, Gustavo. *Gazapo*. Mexico City: Joaquín Mortiz, 1965.

———. *La princesa del palacio de hierro*. Mexico City: Joaquín Mortiz, 1974.

San Juan, Manuel H. *El señor gobernador*. Mexico City: Imprenta y Encuadernación de M. Nava, 1901.

Turón, Carlos Eduardo. *Sobre esta piedra*. Mexico City: Oasis, 1981.

Valdovinos Garza, José. *El hombre que fue dos*. Mexico City: Catalina, 1963.

Zamora Plowes, Leopoldo. *Quince uñas y Casanova, aventureros: Novela histórica picaresca*. 2 vols. Mexico City: Talleres Gráficos de *La nación*, 1945.

Zapata, Luis. *Las aventuras, desventuras y sueños de Adonís García, El vampiro de la colonia Roma*. Mexico City: Grijalbo, 1979.

THEORY AND CRITICISM CITED

Abreu Gómez, Ermilo. Review of *El Canillitas*, by Artemio de Valle-Arizpe. *Letras de México*, 15 July 1941, 5.

Acevedo, Roberto Maximiano. "Vida y obra de Artemio de Valle-Arizpe." Ph.D. diss., University of Arizona, 1972.

Adams, Percy G. *Travel Literature and the Evolution of the Novel.* Lexington: The University Press of Kentucky, 1983.

Alegría, Fernando. *Breve historia de la novela hispanoamericana.* Mexico City: Ediciones de Andrea, 1959.

Anderson Imbert, Enrique. *Spanish-American Literature: A History.* Translated by John V. Falconieri. Detroit: Wayne State University Press, 1963.

Arreola Cortés, Raúl. "José Rubén Romero; vida y obra." *Revista Hispánica Moderna* 12 (1946): 7–34.

Bancroft, Robert L. "The *Periquillo Sarniento* and *Don Catrín de la Fachenda:* Which is the Masterpiece?" *Revista Hispánica Moderna* 34 (1968): 533–38.

Bandelier, Fanny. Introduction to *The Journey of Alvar Núñez Cabeza de Vaca and his Companions from Florida to the Pacific, 1528–1536,* by Alvar Núñez Cabeza de Vaca. New York: Allerton Book Co., 1922.

Barrera, Trinidad. Introduction to *Naufragios,* by Alvar Núñez Cabeza de Vaca. Madrid: Alianza Editorial, 1985.

Barthes, Roland. *S/Z: An Essay.* New York: Hill and Wang, 1974.

Baskett, James Newton. "A Study of the Route of Cabeza de Vaca." *The Texas Historical Quarterly* 10.1 (1907): 246–79; 10.2 (1907): 308–40.

Bellogín García, Andrés. *Vida y hazañas de Alvar Núñez Cabeza de Vaca.* Madrid: Editorial Voluntad, 1982.

Bishop, Morris. *The Odyssey of Cabeza de Vaca.* New York: The Century Co., 1933.

Bjornson, Richard. *The Picaresque Hero in European Fiction.* Madison: University of Wisconsin Press, 1977.

Blackburn, Carol Roark. "The Picaresque Novel of Mexico." Ph.D. diss., University of Illinois, 1969.

Borgeson, Paul W., Jr. "Problemas de técnica narrativa en dos *novellas* de Lizardi." *Hispania* 69 (1986): 504–11.

Brushwood, John S. *Genteel Barbarism.* Lincoln: University of Nebraska Press, 1981.

———. *Mexico in Its Novel: A Nation's Search for Identity.* Austin: University of Texas Press, 1966.

———. *La novela mexicana (1967–1982).* Mexico City: Grijalbo, 1984.

Campbell, Camilla. *Galleons Sail Westward.* Dallas: Mathis, Van Nort and Co., 1939.

Casas de Faunce, María. *La novela picaresca latinoamericana.* Madrid: Cupsa, 1977.

Castagnaro, R. Anthony. "Rubén Romero and the Novel of the Mexican Revolution." *Hispania* 36 (1953): 300–4.

Castagnino, Raúl H. "Carlos de Sigüenza y Góngora o la picaresca a la inversa." In *Escritores hispanoamericanos, desde otros ángulos de simpatía,* 91–101. Buenos Aires: Editorial Nova, 1971.

Cerdán, Willebaldo Bazarte. "La Primera Novela Mexicana." *Humanismo* 7 (1958): 88–107.

Chandler, Frank W. *Romances of Roguery: An Episode in the History of the Novel, The Picaresque Novel in Spain.* New York: Columbia University Press, 1899.

Chang-Rodríguez, Raquel. "La transgresión de la picaresca en los *Infortunios de Alonso Ramírez*." In *Violencia y subversión en la prosa colonial hispanoamericana, siglos XVI y XVII,* 85–108. Madrid: José Porrúa Turanzas, 1982.

Coopwood, Bethel. "Route of Cabeza de Vaca in Texas." *The Texas Historical Quarterly* 3 (1899): 108–40.

Covey, Cyclone. Introduction to *Adventures in the Unknown Interior of America,* by Alvar Núñez Cabeza de Vaca. New York: Collier Books, 1961.

Cumberland, Charles C. *Mexico: The Struggle for Modernity.* London: Oxford University Press, 1968.

Cummins, James S. "The Philippines Glimpsed in the First Latin-American 'Novel'." *Philippine Studies* 26 (1978): 91–101.

———. "*Infortunios de Alonso Ramírez:* 'A Just History of Fact'?" *Bulletin of Hispanic Studies* 61 (1984): 295–303.

Curcio Altamar, Antonio. "La ausencia de novela en el Nuevo Reino." In *La novela hispanoamericana,* 51–59. Compiled by Juan Loveluck. 3rd ed. Chile: Editorial Universitaria, 1969.

Davis, Jack Emory. "Algunos problemas lexicógrafos en *El Periquillo Sarniento.*" *Revista Iberoamericana* 45 (1958): 163–71.

———. "Picturesque 'americanismos' in the works of Fernández de Lizardi." *Hispania* 44 (1961): 74–81.

Davison, Ned J. "La composición de *La vida inútil de Pito Pérez.*" In *Sobre Eduardo Barrios y otros: estudios y crónicas,* 13–17. Albuquerque, N.M.: Foreign Books, 1966.

De Grazia, Ted Ettore. *De Grazia Paints Cabeza de Vaca: The First Non-Indian in Texas, New Mexico, and Arizona 1527–1536.* Tucson: University of Arizona Press, 1973.

Dowling, Lee W. "Story vs. Discourse in the Chronicle of the Indies: Alvar Núñez Cabeza de Vaca's *Relación.*" *Hispanic Journal* 5 (1984): 89–99.

Englekirk, John E., and others. *An Outline History of Spanish American Literature.* 3rd ed. New York: Appleton-Century-Crofts, 1965.

Fernández, José B. *Alvar Núñez Cabeza de Vaca: The Forgotten Chronicler.* Miami: Ediciones Universal, 1975.

———. "Opposing Views of La Florida—Alvar Núñez Cabeza de Vaca and el Inca Garcilaso de la Vega." *Florida Historical Quarterly* 40 (1976): 170–80.

Flores, Angel. *Historia y Antología del Cuento y la Novela en Hispanoamérica.* New York: Las Américas Publishing Co., 1959.

———. *The Literature of Spanish America.* 4 vols. New York: Las Américas, 1966.

Foster, David William. *Mexican Literature: A Bibliography of Secondary Sources.* Metuchen, N.J.: The Scarecrow Press, 1981.

Friedman, Edward H. "The Marginated Narrator: *Hasta no verte Jesús mío* and the Eloquence of Repression." In *The Antiheroine's Voice: Narrative Discourse and the Transformation of the Picaresque,* 170–187. Columbia: University of Missouri Press, 1987.

Galeota, Vito. "Appunti per un'analisi letteraria di *Naufragios* di Alvar Núñez Cabeza de Vaca." *Annali Instituto Universitario Orientales Napoli-Sezione Romanza* 25 (1983): 471–97.

García Márquez, Gabriel. "The Solitude of Latin America." *New York Times*. 6 February 1983. Section IV: 17.

García Rivas, Heriberto. *Historia de la literatura mexicana*. 2 vols. Mexico City: Textos Universitarios, 1971.

Genette, Gérard. *Narrative Discourse: An Essay in Method*. Translated by Jane E. Lewin. Ithaca: Cornell University Press, 1980.

González, Aníbal. *"Los infortunios de Alonso Ramírez:* Picaresca e historia." *Hispanic Review* 51 (1983): 189–204.

González, Manuel Pedro. *Trayectoria de la novela en México*. Mexico City: Botas, 1951.

González Peña, Carlos. *Historia de la literatura mexicana: Desde los orígenes hasta nuestros días*. 9th ed. Mexico City: Porrúa, 1966.

González y Contreras, Gilberto. *El hombre que supo ver.* La Habana, Cuba: La Verónica, 1940.

Greene, Bob. "Bo Schembechler could take a page from Woody's book." *Detroit Free Press*. 31 October 1989. Section B: 11.

Guillén, Claudio. "Toward a Definition of the Picaresque." In *Literature as System: Essays Toward the Theory of Literary History,* 71–106. Princeton: Princeton University Press, 1971.

Hall, Oakley. *The Children of the Sun.* New York: Atheneum, 1983.

Hallenbeck, Cleve. *Alvar Núñez Cabeza de Vaca: the Journey and Route of the First European to Cross the Continent of North America, 1534–1536.* Glendale, Calif.: The Arthur H. Clark Company, 1940.

Hancock, Joel. "Elena Poniatowska's *Hasta no verte Jesús mío:* the Remaking of the Image of Woman." *Hispania* 66 (1983): 353–59.

Hart, Billy T. "A Critical Edition with a Study of the Style of *La relación* by Núñez Cabeza de Vaca." Ph.D. diss., University of Southern California, 1974.

Helí Hernández, Jesús. *Antecedentes Italianos de la Novela Picaresca Española: Aspectos Literarios y Lingüísticos.* Madrid: Ediciones José Porrúa Turanzas, 1982.

Henderson, Walter Brooks Drayton. *The new Argonautica, an heroic poem in eight cantos, of the voyage among the stars of the immortal spirits of Sir Walter Raleigh, Sir Francis Drake, Ponce de Leon and Nuñez da Vaca . . .* New York: The Macmillan Co., 1928.

Holzapfel, Tamara. "Soledad y rebelión en *La vida inútil de Pito Pérez.*" *Revista iberoamericana* 89 (1974): 681–87.

Johnson, Julie Greer. "Picaresque Elements in Carlos Sigüenza y Góngora's *Los infortunios de Alonso Ramírez.*" *Hispania* 64 (1981): 60–67.

Lacalle, Carlos. *Noticia sobre Alvar Núñez Cabeza de Vaca: Hazañas americanas de un caballero andaluz.* Madrid: Instituto de Cultura Hispánica, 1961.

Lafarga, Gastón. *La evolución literaria de Rubén Romero.* Paris: Gouyardín, 1939.

Lagmanovich, David. "Los *Naufragios* de Alvar Núñez como construcción narrativa." *Kentucky Romance Quarterly* 25 (1978): 27–37.

———. "Para una Caracterización de *Infortunios de Alonso Ramírez.*" *Sin Nombre* 5 (1974): 7–14.

Lastra, Pedro. "Espacios de Alvar Núñez: Las transformaciones de una escritura." *Revista chilena de literatura* 23 (1984) 89–102.

Leal, Luis. "Picaresca hispanoamericana: de Oquendo a Lizardi." In *Estudios de literatura hispanoamericana en honor a José A. Arrom*, 47–58. Edited by Andrew P. Debicki and Enrique Pupo-Walker. Chapel Hill: University of North Carolina, 1974.

———. "Pícaros y léperos en la narrativa mexicana." In *La picaresca: orígenes, textos y estructuras*, 1033–40. Edited by Manuel Criado de Val. Madrid: Fundación Universitaria Española, 1979.

Lemaitre, Monique J. "Jesusa Palancares y la dialéctica de la emancipación femenina." *Revista Iberoamericana* 51 (1985): 751–63.

Lewis, Robert E. "Los *Naufragios* de Alvar Núñez: historia y ficción." *Revista Iberoamericana* 48 (1982): 681–94.

Long, Haniel. Introduction to *The Power Within Us: Cabeza de Vaca's Relation of His Journey from Florida to the Pacific 1528–1536*, by Alvar Núñez Cabeza de Vaca. (Partial translation.) New York: Duell, Sloan and Pearce, 1944.

Luchting, Wolfgang A. Review of *El Chanfalla* by Gonzalo Martré. *World Literature Today* 54 (1980): 258.

Miller, Stuart. *The Picaresque Novel*. Cleveland, Ohio: The Press of Case Western Reserve University, 1967.

Moore, Ernest Richard. *Novelistas de la revolución mexicana: José Rubén Romero*. La Habana, Cuba: La Verónica, 1940.

Morton, F. Rand. "José Rubén Romero." In *Los novelistas de la revolución mexicana*, 71–94. Mexico City: Cultura, 1949.

Panger, Daniel. *Black Ulysses*. Athens, Ohio: Ohio University Press, 1982.

Parker, Alexander A. *Literature and the Delinquent: The Picaresque Novel in Spain and Europe 1599–1753*. Edinburgh: Edinburgh University Press, 1967.

Pawlowski, John. "*Periquillo* and *Catrín*: Comparison and Contrast." *Hispania* 58 (1975): 830–42.

Pérez, Galo René. *Historia crítica de la novela hispanoamericana*. Bogotá: Círculo de Lectores, 1977.

Pérez Blanco, Lucrecio. "Novela ilustrada y desmitificación de América." *Cuadernos Americanos* 41 (1982): 176–95.

Phillips, Ewart E. "The Genesis of Pito Pérez." *Hispania* 47 (1964): 698–702.

Poniatowska, Elena. "Hasta no verte, Jesús mío." *Vuelta* 24 (November 1978): 5–11.

"El premio nacional del periodismo por primera vez concedido a una mujer." *Fem* 2.6 (1978) 29.

Purchas, Samuel. *His Pilgrimes*. London: 1613.

Ramos, Samuel. *El perfil del hombre y la cultura en México*. Colección Austral, no. 1180. Mexico City: Espasa Calpe, 1951.

Rosenberg, Sandra. "Travel Literature and the Picaresque Novel." *Enlightenment Essays* 2 (1971): 40–47.

Schembechler, Bo, and Mitch Albom. *Bo*. New York: Warner Books, 1989.

Shklovsky, Victor. "Art as Technique." In *Russian Formalist Criticism*, 3–24. Translated by Lee T. Lemon and Marion J. Reis. Lincoln: University of Nebraska Press, 1965.

Slaughter, Frank G. *Apalachee Gold: The Fabulous Adventures of Cabeza de Vaca*. Garden City, N.Y.: Doubleday, 1954.

Smith, Bradley. *Mexico: A History in Art*. New York: Doubleday, 1968.

Smith, Buckingham, translator. *Shipwrecks of Alvar Núñez Cabeza de Vaca*. By Alvar Núñez Cabeza de Vaca. Washington: 1851. Published for private distribution by George W. Riggs, Jr.

Solís, Emma. *Lo picaresco en las novelas de Fernández de Lizardi*. Mexico City: Lima, 1952.

Soons, Alan. "Alonso Ramírez in an Enchanted and a Disenchanted World." *Bulletin of Hispanic Studies* 53 (1976): 201–5.

Spell, Jefferson Rea. *Bridging The Gap*. Mexico City: Libros de México, 1971. Contains *The Life and Works of José Joaquín Fernández de Lizardi*. Philadelphia: University of Pennsylvania, 1931.

————. Introduction to *Don Catrín de la Fachenda* by José Joaquín Fernández de Lizardi. Mexico City: Cultura, 1944.

————. Prologue to *Don Catrín de la Fachenda y Noches tristes y día alegre*, by José Joaquín Fernández de Lizardi. Mexico City: Porrúa, 1959.

Téllez, Hernando. "La novela en Latinoamérica." In *La novela hispanoamericana*, 44–50. Compiled by Juan Loveluck. 3rd ed. Chile: Editorial Universitaria, 1969.

Terrell, John Upton. *Journey into Darkness: Cabeza de Vaca's Expedition Across North America, 1528–36*. London: Jarrolds, 1964.

Torres-Ríoseco, Arturo. "Humor in Hispanic Literature." In *Aspects of Spanish-American Literature*, 3–30. Seattle: University of Washington Press, 1963.

Trejo Fuentes, Ignacio. "¿Es *El Chanfalla* una novela picaresca?" *Plural* 96 (September 1979): 62–65.

Urdapilleta, Antonio. *Andanzas y desventuras de Alvar Núñez Cabeza de Vaca*. Madrid: Gráficas Valera, 1949.

Usigli, Rodolfo. *El gesticulador*. In Vol. 1 of *Teatro completo de Rodolfo Usigli*, 727–802. Mexico City: Fondo de Cultura Económica, 1963.

Vallés Formosa, Alba. Introduction to *Infortunios de Alonso Ramírez*, by Carlos de Sigüenza y Góngora. San Juan, Puerto Rico: Editorial Cordillera, 1967.

Vogeley, Nancy. "Defining the 'Colonial Reader': *El Periquillo Sarniento*." *PMLA*, 102 (1987): 784–800.

Whitbourn, Christine J. "Moral Ambiguity in the Spanish Picaresque Tradition." In *Knaves and Swindlers: Essays on the Picaresque Novel in Europe*, 1–24. London: Oxford University Press, 1974.

Wicks, Ulrich. "The Nature of Picaresque Narrative: A Modal Approach." *PMLA*, 89 (1974): 240–49.

————. "Onlyman." *Mosaic*, 8 (1975): 21–47.

Williams, O. W. "The Route of Cabeza de Vaca in Texas." *Texas Historical Association Quarterly* 3 (1899): 54–64.

Wojciechowska, Maia. *Odyssey of Courage: The Story of Alvar Núñez Cabeza de Vaca*. New York: Atheneum, 1965.

Index